A
HISTORY OF
HUNGARIAN
MUSIC

Issued as a
" Musical Standard " Extra.

For List of Musical Works
please refer to the end
of the volume.

A
HISTORY OF
HUNGARIAN
MUSIC

BY
JULIUS KALDY,
(DIRECTOR OF THE ROYAL HUNGARIAN OPERA)

LONDON :
WILLIAM REEVES,
The " Musical Standard " Office,
83, Charing Cross Road W C.

HASKELL HOUSE PUBLISHERS Ltd.
Publishers of Scarce Scholarly Books
NEW YORK. N. Y. 10012
1969

First Published 1902

\HASKELL HOUSE PUBLISHERS Ltd.
Publishers of Scarce Scholarly Books
280 LAFAYETTE STREET
NEW YORK. N. Y. 10012

Library of Congress Catalog Card Number: 68-25291

Standard Book Number 8383-0305-6

A

HISTORY OF HUNGARIAN MUSIC.

BY

JULIUS KALDY,

(DIRECTOR OF THE ROYAL HUNGARIAN OPERA)

LONDON :
WILLIAM REEVES,
The "Musical Standard" Office,
83, Charing Cross Road, W.C.

This little work, issued as a MUSICAL STANDARD extra, is Reprinted from " The Millennium of Hungary and Its People,' * by permission of the Editor, Dr. Joseph de Jekelfalussy, Director of the Royal Hungarian Statistical Office and Ministeral Councillor.

* Published under the authority of the Royal Hungarian Minister of Commerce. Budapest.

A HISTORY
* * OF * * *
HUNGARIAN
MUSIC * * *

THE Hungarians must have had a special love for music in their original home, for in their sacrifices and other religious ceremonies, in their national festivals, before and after a battle, at banquets and funerals, Song, Music, and Dancing played an important rôle.

In religious sacrifices the High priest (Táltos) led the ceremony with Song. The people, repeating the last verse of the stanza, softly sang the refrain, and young girls, scattering fragrant herbs in the

A

altar flame, danced a blithe dance. At national festivals and at banquets the minstrels sang, accompanying themselves on their lute, the heroic deeds of fallen champions, or poured forth other patriotic songs, while reciters declaimed in sonorous rhythms the old heroic legends.

Our ancestors used to inter their dead with song and music. Priests of lower rank (Gyulas) delivered an address at the funeral, praised the heroism and virtues of the dead, and at the end paced round the grave in a slow dance. This custom likewise remained partially until the present day. For at burials—with Catholic and Protestant alike—the Cantor takes leave of the dead in a mournful song. After the interment the mourners assemble with the sorrowing family at the funeral banquet. 160 years ago the "Dance of Death" used to be danced after this evening meal.

This was probably the oldest Hungarian dance, which our people here danced for hundreds of years as a remnant of heathen funeral rites. Among the compositions of the renowned Gipsy musician, Czinka Panna, there is a " Dance of Death " melody, of the first half of the 18th century.

That music and song were in great maturity already among the Huns is proved by the Travels of Priscus Rhetor whom the Emperor of Byzantium sent along with the Senator Maximus on an embassy to Attila.

Like the Gallic bards, the Vates, and the Skandinavian Skalds, the Hun minstrels not only stimulated the fighters to the combat but took part in the battle themselves. Many of them remained on the field of battle. In 451, on the eve of the bloody and desperate battle of Catalaunum, when Attila withdrew to his barricade of waggons, the dirges of the Huns echoed from there to the enemy's camp. Next day numberless lutes were found on the battle-field.

Later, at the time of the conquest of the land, in the 10th century, the music of the Hungarians must have been highly developed, for the "Anonymous" of King Béla (Anonymus Bélæ Regis notarius) ends his account of the fights of the leaders Lel, Bulcsu, and Botond, with the words: "As to their wars and heroic deeds, if you pay no credence to my letter, at least believe the prattling songs of the minstrels, and the well-worn legends of the people, who have not allowed the heroic deeds of the Hungarians up till now to fall into oblivion." After Arpád had conquered the land, he marched with his people into the castle of Attila, where everything was waste and neglected. "In the ruins"—says the Anonymous—"they held daily banquets, they sat in rows in the palace of Attila, and the sounds and sweet tones of their lutes and shalms, and all sorts of songs from their vocalists, echoed from the company.' Along with the Anonymous notary other chroniclers also mention the numerous hymns, dirges and martial songs, the latter of which were forthcoming in great numbers, and enjoyed universal favour.

The minstrels, reciters, and jongleurs can be regarded as the makers of these songs, who already at Arpád's time sang their heroic songs at national festivities, which came into popular use thereby. The name "igricz," of slavic origin, used to refer to Harlequinades, Mummeries, and buffooneries, and since it was not in the nature of the Hungarians to take part in common antics, in frivolous buffooneries, or to feel any particular pleasure therein, it is probable that these jongleurs were of foreign nationality. In their place came the Troubadours later, whose name is by many people derived from " tréfa " (fun).

Many interesting facts about the dance of the Hungarians are found in the Chronicle of the Monk of St. Gallen, Ekkehard (10th century). He relates that in the Hungarian dance there are seven steps. He names it "Siebensprünge" ("the Seven Steps"). This dance was taught to the people of the Lake of Constance by the Hungarians during the latter's residence there, who later under the name of "Hun step" applied this dance to their own slow moving dance.

Many aver that the leaders themselves made the old Hungarian heroic songs, the minstrels being only their exponents, after having put them to music.

All testimony points to the fact that at Arpád's time music was not only beloved by great personages, but also among the people. It is known of Bishop Gerhard, that, when he came from his seat Csanád with Walther, the singing-master of the Fehérvár School, to King Stephen I., he passed the night on the way at suitable places, and through the night was awakened from his sleep by songs. The bishop turned to his conductor with the words

" Walther, do you hear how sweet the song of the Hungarians is ? " Since the songs grew clearer and clearer, Gerhard continued : " Walther, tell me, what causes this song which compels me to interrupt my slumbers ? " On this, Walther declared that a girl was the singer, who ground wheat on a handmill and whiled away her hard work with singing. Thus the Hungarians had already at that time a taste for singing, and carried on their hard work while singing, just as at present, when the most beautiful Hungarian folk-songs arise at ploughing and sowing, at the harvest and the vintage.

The Hungarian music must have had great repute even 800 years ago, for when the Hungarians fought as allies of the Russian prince Isislav, against the Poles and Bohemians, and, after a victorious fight, marched with triumphal pomp into Kiev, the townspeople got up festivities in honour of their guests, and "the house was fortunate in which Hungarian music sounded."

We know from descriptions that the following instruments were in use in Hungary: the Lute (koboz, a kind of Indian Lyre), and the Violin (hegedü) likewise a string-instrument. Of wind-instruments, large and small pipes were made out of willow twigs—which are still a popular instrument like the Shepherd's pipe (*tilinkó*) ;—the horn made out of the buffalo or ox's horn called " kürt "; the small hand-drum, like a Moorish tambourine, but without castanets. It is best to assume that the Hungarians brought these musical instruments from their original home. The field-trumpet and the cymbal were of later date.

With regard to form, opinions about the old lutes are various. Most probably it was like the Indian national instrument, the *Vina*. The player sat, laid it on his knee, and played *pizzicato*. Among the Székelys, in Transylvania, there is still a

similar instrument which is so played
and is called the "timbora."

Unfortunately we know not a single
melody from the music of the Huns'
songs, nor from the time of the old
heathenism, but from the manner of life
and the continual wars of our people it is
self-evident that the music of that time
must have been dramatic and heroic.
The best proof of its once high development are the old Hungarian legends and
traditions, which relate in song the fortunate or unfortunate careers of the nation, the heroic deeds of Attila, Arpád,
and the dukes. The melodies of these
songs were gradually lost in the advance
of Christianity, and it is probable that,
with the crushing of Vata's rebellion,
very many precious poetical and musical
products of the ancient days of heathen
Hungary were entirely destroyed.

Under Stephen I., and later, the Christian church-music spread also among us,
and the Gregorian song soon took root

here, too, as among all the other proselytes
to Christianity. The schools founded by
Stephen I. and his successors had a two-
fold task : to educate in Christian religion
and in song.

In the first of these schools founded be
Bishop Gregory at Székesfehérvár, the
forementioned Walther instructed the
children of thirty christianised families in
Latin and in song.

Several bishops followed this example,
and thus schools arose in Esztergom,
Pannonhalma, Vácz, Veszprém, Nagy-
várad and Nyitra.

The church-music had some influence
on our popular songs is plain from certain
Folk-songs whose melody is constructed
on the Scale of Church-music, which at
the same time is a convincing proof of
their age. In these songs, though the
words are more recent, the melodies
plainly show the influence of Christian
Church-music.

Since the first priests in Hungary were

strangers and principally Italians, as a matter of course they taught the young people only Latin songs. Later, when several natives became clergymen, they spread the Church-songs in Hungarian translations, composed church-songs themselves, Hymns with Hungarian text which, however, by a law of King Kálmán's time (1112) could only be adopted among Church-songs on approval by the Synod.

Our annals mention several such composers of this time, among the rest Andreas Vásárhelyi, who wrote a song to the Virgin as Patroness of Hungary, and an unknown composer, whose song on St. Stephen was printed at Nüremburg in 1454.

From this time the Hungarian text of another church song has come down to us, the Königsberg fragment " On the virginity of the Virgin Mary." The tunes of the three songs mentioned we do not know, but they cannot have been aught else than the ordinary Gregorian Hymns.

We must now mention two pre-eminent Hungarians, who have acquired European renown by their art. The first was Nicolas Klinsor in the 13th Century, a Transylvanian who lived at the court of Andreas III., and as one of the most learned of the Master Singers took part in the competition held at the Wartburg near Eisenach in 1208 at the invitation of the German Minnesinger, Henry von Ofterdingen. Some of his songs are found in the old epic poem : Der Sängerkrieg auf der Wartburg (the singing match at the Wartburg). Still more famous was George Szlatkoni (Slakoni, Slakona), born in Krajna near Nyitra, 1456, who at the beginning of the 16th century was the 4th bishop of St. Stephen's church in Vienna, and as privy councillor and choir-master to Emperor Maximilian I. distinguished himself in religious and secular music alike.*)

---

* Among the pictures of Hans Burgmayer (Imperial and Royal Library, Vienna) which contain

At the court of the Hungarian Kings of mixed families foreign masters often found employment. The Capellmeister of King Sigismund was the renowned Georg Stolzer, Josquin des Prés' contemporary. At the court of King Mathias, the great Netherland theorist, Johann Tinctoris, resided, who was the Capellmeister of King Ferdinand of Naples and the music-master of his daughter Beatrice. Beatrice brought him with her to Hungary, and

---

135 woodcuts and exhibit the triumph of the Emperor Maximilian, our countryman is portrayed sitting in a cant equipage and directing his band of singers and musicians. Under the picture is the word "Apollo." The explanation appended to the pictures thus alludes to Szlakoni :

Szlakoni (Bishop in Vienna) is to be made Capellmeister, and the rhyme has reference to the fact, that, by direction of the Emperor, he arranged the singing of the choir in a most charming manner :

In consonance and harmony,
In melody and symphony,
In every art to my desire
Have I improved the tuneful choir.
And yet the honour not to me
But to my Emperor must be.

under him the court-band and the singers
of King Matthias attained world-wide
renown. According to Peter, Bishop of
Vulturan and legate of Sixtus IV., there
was no better choir at that time than that
of King Matthias.

This fact plainly shows that King
Matthias fostered music, and that the
Queen as well as he had a band and a
choir. In addition there was a well-
organized band of trumpets. The band
of the King and Queen must have consisted of 30 executants, which was
reckoned an extraordinary number for
that time, if we compare the Vienna band
of Leopold some centuries later, which was
only 18 strong.

Tinctoris dedicated to Queen Beatrice
one of his renowned theoretical works.
At the same time lived Monetarius, born
at Selmecz, who distinguished himself as
a composer and by a theoretical work,
which he dedicated to George Thurzó in
1513.

Even King Wladislaus II., renowned for his great poverty, spent 200 pieces of gold yearly on his singers and musicians.

Under Lewis II. Adrian Willaert, of Netherland birth (afterwards the founder of the Venetian School), lived seven years at Buda, and left Hungary after the battle of Mohács. Willaert, the creator of the Madrigal, dedicated to the wife of Lewis II. a madrigal consisting of several parts, which is preserved in St. Mark's Library at Venice.

The residence of these illustrious personages in our land, who were all disciples of the old counterpoint, has exercised small influence on the character of the Hungarian music, for singers and instruments alike were brought sometimes out of Italy, sometimes from Germany, and, while they figured as court musicians only in churches and at court festivities, Hungarian music drew little advantage from their sojourn here and only a few popular songs have descended to us, e.g., the song " Mátyást

mostan választotta " (King Matthias has
been elected) which the children sang at
Matthias' election to the throne.

In King Sigismund's time there were
organs in many churches. There is a
well known document of John Hunyadi
(1452) in which the parish of Felsö-Bánya
is allowed certain expenses for the erec-
tion of an organ. The first introduction
of this instrument, however, cannot be
historically indicated. According to
Nicolas Oláh an organ with silver pipes
was played at Visegrád in the chapel of
King Matthias, whereas at Buda Masses
with song were celebrated ; thus not only
was the royal Cathedral (Matthias' church)
decorated with an organ, but there was
also instrumental music corresponding to
the time.

With regard to the Hungarian Folk-
songs and Dance Music, no certain data
have come down to us from these centuries: * still we may assume that it went on

---

* The 10th to the 15th centuries.

a way of its own despite foreign influence. Conspicuous executants of Hungarian dance-music were the wandering gipsies of the 14th century, and they especially spread the Hungarian secular instrumental music. Not only the people patronized them, but they were willingly entertained at the courts of the magnates. They played a rôle not only in festivities, but sometimes also at the Parliament meetings, of which our historians make mention, at the noisy assemblies at Rákos and Hatvan in 1525. The most conspicuous was Dominik Kármán who, according to Tinódi, enjoyed great renown as a lutist and a violinist. A verse of Tinódi testifies that the lute at that time was played by the fingers, but the violin was already played by the gipsies with the bow.

In the 18th century Michael Barna and Czinka Panna, distinguished themselves —the former being called the Hungarian Orpheus—on whose life and death numer-

B

ous Latin poems were written. Johann
Bihary followed them, one of the most
illustrious, whose recruiting tunes and
Primate, Palatine, and *Coronation* tunes are
among the most beautiful of Hungarian
dances. He and his band were invited
more than once to the Court-balls at
Vienna. He gave concerts in Hungary,
Transylvania, Poland, and Vienna; the
great Beethoven listened to his playing
often with great pleasure, and has used
the melody of a slow Hungarian tune of
Bihary's in his overture dedicated to
King Stephen. At present our gipsy
bands win laurels not only in Europe
but also in America and Asia, reaping
both money and renown. They deserve
our thanks for spreading Hungarian
music.

Returning to earlier centuries, we must
not forget war-songs and camp-music.
History mentions as composers of this
style John Cesinge, who, as Bishop of
Pécs (15th century), placed himself at the

head of his troops, and inspired his soldiers to battle by his songs. ✓ Several Hungarian lutists had repute in Europe already in the 16th century. One was Valentine Bakfark, others say Graevisius (born in Transylvania 1507, died at Padua 1576), who lived chiefly in Poland. He came at the invitation of the emperor Maximilian to Vienna (1570) where he played a rôle at court. He lived long at the court of the Polish King August Sigismund, with whom he must have been on intimate terms, at least the preface of one of his works says as much. Two of his works have come down to us: Premier livre de tabulature de lutte (Paris, 1564), and Bakfarci Valentini Greffi Pannonii Harmoniarum musicarum usum testudinis factorum (Cracoviæ, 1566). He dedicated the last work to the Polish King, who bestowed on him a property as leader of the court band. ✓John Bakfark—probably son of the foregoing—was also a lute virtuoso of great fame. Among the works of both we find several compositions written in Hungarian style.

As excellent lutist must be named John Newsidler, who was born in Pozsony. His school for the Lute appeared in Nuremberg. In the first volume of this work he treats of Lute tablature. In the second volume are several Fantasias, Preludes, Psalms and Motetts.

A contemporary of his was Christopher Armpruster, also born in Transylvania, whose Pamphlet, "Song on morality," appeared in print in 1551.

In the 16th century are conspicuous Andreas Batizi (1546) with his "Fair history of the Holy Marriage of the Patriarch Isaac," Andreas Farkas (1538) with "How God led Israel's people from Egypt and similarly the Hungarians from Scythia," Peter Kákonyi, Peter Désy, Kasper Bajnai, Stephan Csükei, Michael Sztáray, Blasius Székely, and Michael Tarjay, who have also written songs with biblical purport, and whose style despite their religious character, is quite Hungarian. In the airs there is much melodious invention. Many a song sounds just like an earnest slow Hungarian tune. We see, therefore, how, even in the 16th century, those who were of pure Hungarian race were concerned with music and aimed at elevating our national music not only in secular songs, but by applying it to religious ditties.

At this time Sebastian Tinódi lived, the lute-player of the 16th century, whom the people named " Sebök-deák." He was the prototype of the true lutist, wandering through the country, and playing his lute here and there. He wrote music to his songs. He was not only a true chronicler in his historical songs of the events of the 16th century, but he was the first Hungarian composer; for the musical invention of his songs and their construction are of quite a Hungarian character, and some of his songs, *e.g.* " Sok csudák " (Many a miracle),

" Siess keresztyén " (Hasten Christian)
are quite unique and possess abiding
worth. The tune of his song " Enyingi
Török " Francis Erkel has adapted in his
famous funeral march in his opera " Ladislaus Hunyadi."

Tinódi's songs passed from mouth to
mouth at that time, and people began
afterwards to perpetuate their style, as
the numerous songs and ballads of the
Thököly and Rákóczy period show.

The bloom of Hungarian music, however,
began to take greater dimensions already
with the spread of the Hungarian Reform-
ation. Then the people sang in churches
in their own language, and made their
musical forms out of the tunes in the
Psalter. At that time secular poems
were often sung to the music of sacred
songs, and in many tunes composed in
the 17th century we recognise the tunes
of the hymns of the Huguenots composed by Gaudimel which were natural-
ized with us.

The most brilliant period of our Folk-songs is in the time of Thököly and still more in that of Rákóczy. We can only wonder at the beauty, impressiveness, natural strength and characteristic rhythm of the so-called *Kurutz songs* and be amazed at their variety.

The Kurutz songs and other musical creations of that time are not only genuine musical pearls, but accurately reflect, also, the character and peculiarity of the Hungarian music and form the source from which the later songs, tunes, recruiting songs, wedding and other dances, and the whole body of the so-called "hallgató magyar" melodies have sprung. If we take into consideration that the great masters, Handel and Sebastian Bach, were born, or in their childhood, when these songs arose, and that Haydn, Mozart, Beethoven—this triad of geniuses—lived 50 or 60 years later, we can scarcely express our marvel at the astonishing variety and versatility of the bold forms and richness of the rhythm which had revealed itself in Hungarian music at the end of the 17th and the beginning of the 18th century. F. Liszt rightly remarks: "There is no other music from which European musicians can learn so much rhythmic originality as the Hungarian."

At this time arose "Rákóczi Ferencz dala" (Song of Francis Rákóczi), "Rákóczi siralma" (Rákóczi's complaint), and the "Rákóczi nóta" (Rákóczi Tune), from which the world-renowned Rákóczi March sprang a hundred years later.

At this period were composed the numerous melancholy songs of the exiles: "Oszi harmat" (Autumnal dew), "Ne búsulj" (Don't be grieved), "Adam Balogh's tune" and "Bercsényi's tune" which have enduring value, and also many folk-songs which arose later can be referred to this period, viz., "Repülj fecském" (Fly, my swallow), "Az ég alatt" (Under the heaven), "Vörös bársony süvegem" (My cap of red velvet),

" Zöld asztalon ég a gyertya " (The candle is burning on the green table) ; and many other famous songs date from the Rákóczi period.

From the middle of the 17th to the end of the 18th century, only the Song and the Tune (nóta) were known in Hungarian music. The Song was a simple Folk-song, a war-song or a hymn. By "Tune" was implied a piece of music of greater extent. There was already, as we said, Thököli, Rákóczi, Bercsényi Tunes, from which sprang later the so-called " hallgató magyar," melodies which were intended for public performance. Also the different styles of Hungarian Dance-music arose in this period.

We had two sorts of dances, Court dances and Peasant dances. The "Palace dance" and the "Slow Hungarian" were court dances, the " Dance tune " and the " Dumping tune " were Peasant dances. The old Palace Dance was known exclusively as a court dance in the 15th century.

Its music is quite different from the difficult tempoed music of its time, and from the later foreign dances: Saraband, Pavan and Minuet. Its melody was livelier and moved in quicker rhythms. The nobility and their ladies danced it; and since it only consisted of slow turns and was rather a walking dance, old ladies and gentlemen, nay, even ecclesiastics, took part in it. In the music of this dance young Knights often showed their cleverness in a Hungarian solo, but at such occasions they moved more rapidly. This dance was danced also abroad as the " Passo mezzo ongarese " or " Passo mezzo ongaro " and formed a separate part of the Italian " Ballo."

From the Palace and the Slow Hungarian Dance rose the " Verbunkos," which was danced at recruiting. No other nation beside the Hungarian possesses such a dance. Popular dances were also the *Lakodalmas* (Wedding-dance), *Incsalkedö* (the " Coquettish "),

Kalákás, which were in use at weddings; the *Sátoros* (Dance of the tents), *Fegyveres* (Dance of the arms), and *Dobogó* (Drumming-dance), which were danced in camps and after the battle.

During the forties of the 19th Century several Hungarian Society dances arose, *e.g.*, the *Körmagyar* (Ronde-magyar), the *Füzér-táncz* (Wreaths-dance), and the *Csárdás* (Tavern-dance), which is still in vogue.

As an excellent dance-composer, John Latova must be mentioned, belonging to the last century, who has written more than 80 works of this class. Antonia Csermák and Markus Rózsavölgyi who has written many excellent dances, followed him.

At the end of the 17th century some of our artists attained celebrity and brought honour to Hungary abroad. One of these was J. Sigismund Cousser, born at Pozsony, who in 1697 at Hamburg helped Mattheson and Kaiser to create the first

German opera. He produced a large number of his operas there. His operas Erindo (1693), Porus (1694), Pyramus and Thisbe (1694), Scipio in Africa (1697), enjoyed great favour. In 1700 he was choirmaster at Dublin Cathedral, where he died about 1730.*

In the sphere of church-music Johann Francisci, born at Beszterczebánya in 1691, attained great honour as an excellent organist. He travelled through Germany, knew Mattheson and J. S. Bach, and had such renown that one of his friends in Breslau, Joh. Glettinger (1725), was inspired to make the following panegyric :

> Illustrious friend, Amphion's progeny ;
> My fancy finds art's true ideal in thee.

---

* The following works appeared in print :— " Apollon enjoué," containing six overtures, " The joy of the Muses " (Nüremberg, 1700), " Ode on the death after renouned Arabella Hunt " (London), " Serenade on the Birthday of the English King. George I.," Dublin (1724).

Tny songs are like an angel's songs above,
And thus the world bestows on thee her love;
This only wish have I at my command,
That thou may'st be the Orpheus of thy land.

In 1733 he was invited to Pozsony,
where he lived as church-choirmaster.
He returned to his native land to a similar
post in 1735.

In the second half of the preceding
century the higher circles cultivated
secular music, especially Italian and
German, to a great degree. They kept excellent bands, and invited to their con-
ductorship illustrious foreign conductors.

The Esterházys' were pre-eminent for
their patronage of music. Duke Nicholas
Esterházy, and afterwards his son Paul,
had in Kis-Marton a theatre erected with
great luxury, and a distinguished band,
at the head of which was Joseph Haydn,
afterwards Ignatz Pleyel, and lastly
Johann Nep. Hummel. The Károlyis had
permanent bands and theatres in Megyer,
the Batthyany's in Rohoncz, and the

Erdödy's in Pozsony. The higher clergy
were not behindhand in the culture of
music and kept in their residences singers
and musicians, placing distinguished
foreign masters at their head, which was
of great influence to the formation of the
Church style and also of secular music.
The illustrious contrapuntist and theorist
Albrechtsberger, Beethoven's master,
lived at Győr, Michael Haydn also and
Karl Dittersdorf in Nagy-Várad. They
all exercised great influence on the development of the musical life in the towns
mentioned. That influence can still be
seen in all the towns where there was a
standing band, for at these places the
taste for music and its encouragement
has remained among the people till the
present day. As examples. let us
quote Kassa, Eger, Nagy-Várad, Pécs,
Pozsony, Temesvár, where an excellent
soil is prepared not only for concerts, but
for theatrical exhibitions. After many
of these bandmasters, musicians and

singers had founded families and remained in our land, the cultivation of
music came more into fashion. Piano-
playing began to spread at the beginning
of this century. There was scarcely a
nobleman's house, where this instrument
was not found. For this reason several
illustrious foreign masters settled in Hungary and occupied themselves with pianoforte teaching. These masters were disciples of Haydn, Mozart, Beethoven, and
thus the piano compositions of these
three geniuses were introduced into
aristocratic circles, where there must have
been excellent players, since Beethoven
has dedicated several of his classical
piano sonatas to Hungarian ladies of high
rank. The taste for music soon spread in
middle-class society, and from this class
proceeded our best musicians and composers. We must thank this movement
for the fact that several Hungarian in-
struction-books appeared at the beginning of the century. The first School for

Piano was written by Stephen Gati (Buda 1809), which was followed by Dömény's and Milovitzkys Piano School, and a course of Harmony entitled the " Hungarian Apollo " by Andreas Bartay.

All these publications had a favourable effect on the development of music in general and that of Hungarian music in particular.

The number of those who cultivated Hungarian music was already considerable.

From their ranks Johann Fuss arose (born Tolna, 1777, died Vienna, 1819) who was so conspicuous as a composer of all styles of music that he awoke the interest of Haydn. He generally lived at Vienna, but in 1800 he was invited to Pozsony as composer, where he received universal esteem. He wrote string quartettes, trios, duos for violin and piano, sonatas for piano, solos and duets, overtures, sacred works and numerous duologues. The greater part of his works are printed.

Two countrymen of ours attained world-wide renown at the beginning of this century—Johann Nep. Hummel (born on Nov. 14th, 1778, at Pozsony), and Franz Liszt (born 22nd October, 1811, at the village of Doborján, in the County of Sopron). Hummel as a pianist belonged to the last cultivation of the classical style, and excelled by his free improvisa-ion. The number of his compositions exceeds 120, of which his concertos for the piano and his renowned Septet for Wind instruments are of abiding worth. He died at Weimar on the 7th of October, 1837. His birth place, Pozsony, erected a statue to his memory in 1888.

Franz Liszt, awoke such wonder by his piano-playing in his 9th year, that he was called the second Mozart. The families of Szapáry, Apponyi, Esterházy, and Erdödy guaranteed a yearly amount for the child's education. His father took him to Vienna, where Charles Czerny and Salieri were his masters. At this

C

time he was introduced to Beethoven
who prophesied a brilliant future for the
boy, and kissed him publicly at his first
concert at Vienna. At the age of 16—17
he ravished the world with his concerts.
At the end of 1848 he abandoned the
rôle of virtuoso, devoted himself to composition and settled in Weimar. There
he began to write his incomparable Hungarian Rhapsodies, 15 in all, in which he
employed the prettiest Folk-songs, and
Dances, and the Rákóczy March. By
his means Hungarian music was spread
and made popular in Europe. He was
the creator of the Rhapsody and of the
Symphonic Poem. In the last named
composition he employed many Hungarian tunes *e.g.* in " Battle of the Huns "
and " Hungaria," and proved hereby that
Hungarian music is capable of being
applied to serious purposes.

We should have to write books in
order to do justice to his many-sidedness
as a composer and to his compositions.

Also as a tone-poet he occupies a high place. He was the apostle of Richard Wagner, who later became his son-in-law, and he paved the way for that great musical reformer.

In 1862, he went to Rome, where he lived in the seclusion of the Convent Monte Maria and there under the title of an Abbé received the lowest clerical ordination. At this time he wrote his most important works, his oratorio, " St. Elizabeth," first performed in Budapest in 1865, his renowned Hungarian Coronation March in 1867 and his oratorio, " Christus," which was first performed in Budapest in 1875. In both of the former he employed many Hungarian melodies.

He was President of the Royal Hungarian Academy of Music in 1875, where he taught the piano to the highest class. He died at Bayreuth on the 31st of July, 1886.

We Hungarians may be proud of the fact that the great gladiators of piano-playing, Hummel and Liszt, were our countrymen.

A worthy contemporary of Liszt's was Francis Erkel (born 5th November, 1810, at Békés-Gyula. Died at Budapest 15th June, 1860). He can be confidently named as the creator of the Hungarian original opera, for all that was produced in this sphere before him by Joseph Rusicska with his " Flight of Béla," Joseph Heinisch with his " Election of King Matthias," and Andreas Bartay with his opera entitled " Cunning," can scarcely be regarded as aught else than as a more or less successful attempt at soaring, although genuine Hungarian music played a considerable part in these works. Francis Erkel's merits on this field are immortal. He showed the path to be followed and the means to be adopted that Hungarian opera might be a worthy companion of foreign musical drama. In 1848 he wrote " Maria Báthori," this was followed by " Ladislaus Hunyadi," which was received with enthusiasm. Individual parts of this opera, the remarkable overture, the swan song, the church scene, the funeral March, can be said to be of classical value in the literature of Hungarian music. In 1860 his " Bánk Bán " was performed. In this work he attained very original and striking effects by the use of the Hungarian cymbal, along with old instruments seldom employed. In the scene on the banks of the Tisza he made the shepherd's pipe sound (of course represented by 2 piccolos) and gives to individual scenes a thoroughly Hungarian character. His opera " Sarolta " was performed in 1862. " George Dóza " followed in 1874, " Nameless Heroes " in 1880, " George Brankovics " in 1874 and " King Stephen " in 1885. The last work he wrote in his 76th year, despite which the melodic invention and instrumentation are as fresh as in his [early ?] works.

He also takes first place as bandmaster.

In his artistic life of more than half a century he laid the foundations of the Philharmonic Concerts in Budapest, in 1850, and conducted them for eighteen years.

We cannot speak with detail of his services as bandmaster but can only mention the fact that it is through him that the orchestra of the National Theatre has gained European renown. His name will always live as the composer of the national hymn "Isten áldd meg a magyart" (God save the Magyar) so long as there is a Hungarian in the land.

As a dramatic composer Charles Goldmark stands in the first rank, who, in the sphere of symphonies, chamber music, and song composition, enjoys a wide reputation not only in his own country but in all the cultivated world. Goldmark was born at Keszthely in 1832. He awoke real enthusiasm in 1860 when he came before the public with his Suite composed for violin and piano and his

Overture " Sakuntala " of eastern character. Goldmark belongs to those pre-
eminent men of talent who distinguish
themselves by originality, feeling, a vein
of poetry, noble inspiration and interesting
harmony.   He is also a master of brilliant
orchestration.   Of his works the most
remarkable are the Symphony " The
Country Wedding," the overtures " Pen-
thesilea,"   " Spring,"   and   " Sappho."
These works are found in the repertoires
of Philharmonic Concerts all the world
over.   He gained the greatest success
with his opera, " The Queen of Sheba "
(1873).   In this work his musical talents
are at their best.   In 1886, thirteen years
later, his opera " Merlin " was performed.
In this he abandoned his eastern style,
and, curbing his individuality, has produced a work of grand style and of noble
melody, which is almost equal to the
" Queen of Sheba."   Of late he has tried
his powers in the lyric sphere, and with
his new opera " A házi tücsök " (Cricket

on the hearth) he has repeatedly shown
his many-sided brilliant talents. His
music has much of Hungarian character
in melody and conception alike.

Goldmark works slowly and re-writes
much, but what he does write, be it a
piece for the piano, a song, an orchestral
piece, or an opera, all stands on a high
level.

In the sphere of opera there are at present Karl Thern, the composer of Vörös-
marty's " Song of Fót," whose operas
" Gizul " and " The Siege of Tihany,"
gained great success in 1840; further,
Charles Huber with his comic opera, "The
Székely Maid," into which he has worked
several of our prettiest songs. Charles
Huber has done much as a violin teacher;
he wrote an excellent violin school into
the practical part of which he has incor-
porated many Hungarian songs. From
his compositions we must single out " 5
Hungarian Fantasias for Violin and
Piano," and many patriotic male choruses,

"Freedom's song," "Memory of our Ancestors," "National flags," "For holy fatherland," "Song of inspiration," etc.

His son Eugene Hubay is one of the most renowned violinists, who enjoys great fame not only in Hungary but abroad. Thus far he has written three operas. "Alienor," and "The Lutanist of Cremona," were first performed in the Royal Hungarian Opera House. With the latter he gained success abroad. Of late he has struck out a new style with his opera "Falu rossza" (The bad fellow of the village)—the so-called popular operetta, which from beginning to end contains the prettiest Hungarian music, while the new arts of modern technique are applied simultaneously.

A very cultivated, fertile, and many-sided man is Edmund Mihalovich. As a composer he is a disciple of the new school. The style of the Symphonic Poem, created by Liszt, he cultivates with success. His works, " Hero and Leander," " La

Ronde du Sabbat," " The ghostly vessel,"
and "Sellö" (Nymph) are all eminent.
His tunes are noble, his orchestration
masterly. Thus far he has written two
operas, "Hagbarth und Signe" and
"Toldi's Love." In Hungarian music
he is very successful, as is proved by his
compositions for orchestra, "Dirge in
memory of Francis Deák," and "Toldi's
Love." Richard Wagner highly es-
teemed his musical talents, and wrote
" Wieland the Smith " for him. Francis
Sárossy has also written the successful
operas " Atala " and " The last Aben-
cerage."

It is a matter for congratulation that
we have talented composers among the
younger generation. One of these is
Emerich Elbert, who has shown dramatic
power in the opera " Tamora "; further
Edmund Farkas whose two operas, " The
Penitents " and " Valentin Balassa," are
written with beautiful melodic invention;
Julius Mannheimer whose opera " Mari-

tana," and Maurice Varinecz whose "Rosamunda " and " Ratclif " have been performed abroad.

As cultivators of Hungarian music we must mention Michael Mosonyi (born in 1814 in Boldogasszonyfalva, county Moson), and Cornelius Abrányi, sen., who have rendered great services in the development of Hungarian music. Mosonyi in the fifties played a leading rôle in Pesth, and was an authority on church and chamber music. He wrote string quartets, Symphonies and religious compositions. In 1850 he applied himself with all his heart to the cultivation of Hungarian music. He gained great success with his pièces de circonstance: The memory of Kazinczy, Széchényi-Mourning, Festive Ouverture, Victory and Grief of the Hungarian Honvéd. The Hungarian ballad, the song, the male and mixed choruses, the Cantata and the opera are beholden to him for excellent works. Among his best works are " The Festival of the old Hungarians at the river Ung " and " Fair Ilona," a romantic Hungarian opera.

As teacher and distinguished musical savant he had excellent scholars, *e.g.*, Alexander Erkel, Julius Erkel, Edmund Mihalovich, Ladislaus Zimay, etc. He died in 1870. Franz Liszt composed a funeral March in his memory.

Cornelius Abrányi played not only an important rôle in the spread of Hungarian music, but as composer he also takes a high place. His songs and ballads for solo voice, his fantasias for piano, are excellent specimens of Hungarian music. He has distinguished himself also as a writer on music. He founded the first Hungarian musical journal. He wrote instruction books, such as A School of Composition, A General History of Music and The Peculiarities of Hungarian Music. He founded at Arad the National Choral Society. The number of his compositions reaches nearly 100.

Edward Bartay has done much for the spread of Hungarian Music. From 1860 he has taken an active part in our musical movements. At present he is director of the National Conservatorium. He has written piano pieces, choruses, and instrumental works, which have been often performed with success. In the cultivation of orchestral and chamber music Julius Beliczay, I. Julius Major, Francis Xav. Szabó, Paul Jámbor, Arpád Késmárky and Isidor Bátor are eminent for many excellent works.

Virtuoso playing which Liszt brought to great perfection has had great exponents also in our country, among them Emerik Székely (born in 1823 at Mátyusfalva, county Ugocsa) must be mentioned. Among his compositions are string quartets, trios and sonatas, but his fame is founded on his 32 Hungarian Fantasias, written for piano, and his 12 music idylls in which he has elaborated the greates treasures of our modern Folk-songs.

Stephen Heller, the illustrious pianist, born at Budapest in 1815, achieved great success in 1830. The number of his works for the piano is 140. They are character-ised by originality, good taste, elegant treatment and richness of melody. Since 1838 he lived at Paris, where he took first rank among distinguished pianoforte teachers, and where he died.*

A Hungarian pianist of European re-nown is Count Géza Zichy, who, in his 14th year, by an unlucky wound from a gun lost his right arm. By unwearied diligence he succeeded in training his left hand so that not only in Hungary but in the whole cultivated world he had excited the greatest admiration by his pianoforte playing. As a composer he has written several songs, many excellent works for choruses and the opera "Alar." He

---

* Stephen Heller, although born at Budapest, was not, however, an Hungarian. His parents were German Jews who had settled in Pesth. ED. MUSICAL STANDARD.

writes almost all the text to his own compositions.

In the composition of Hungarian songs, ballads, and male choruses the principa writers are : Benjamin Egressy the author of the melody of the " Szózat," with his noble popular songs ; Ladislaus Zimay, Victor Langer, Ernest Lányi, with their romances ; Alexander Erkel, the distinguished bandmaster, with his patriotic male choruses ; Francis Gaál and Alois Tarnay. With our musical literature there is closely connected a species of Hungarian drama, the Popular Play, which takes its subjects from common life and which has the Folk-song and the dance as one of its principal elements. Edward Szigligety was the creator of this style of art. To his first two pieces, " Szökött Katona " (The Deserter), and " Csikós " (The Coltherd), Josef Szerdahelyi wrote the music, using for that purpose our oldest and most original songs. Also the music to " Matyás Diák " (The

student Matthias), Bányarém" (The
terror of the mine), "Liliomfi" is written
by him. Later writers of the same order
are Benjamin Egressy, Ignaz Bognár,
Julius Káldy, Julius Erkel, Alexander
Nikolits. Executants in this branch are
Mimi de Cau, Michel Füredy, Josef
Tamásy, Madame Hegedüs, and Madame
Blaha. This style of drama greatly con-
tributed to the fact that popular Hungarian music became known and appreciated
abroad, for our publishers, directly after
the performance of a piece, published the
prettiest songs in it and circulated them not
only in Hungary but also in Europe, so
as to admit of foreign composers familiar-
ising themselves with Hungarian music.

We should have to write a regular
anthology if we reckoned up all the compositions which famous foreign composers
have written in the Hungarian style, or
in which they have used Hungarian songs.
In the works of Haydn, Beethoven, Schubert, and Weber we find many Hungarian

passages. We can mention only a few of the later composers, and thus we may credit Berlioz with the transcription of the renowned Rákóczy march ; Volkmann with " Visegrád," Twelve sketches for piano called " Hungarian sketches," " Souvenir of Maroth ; " " At the tomb Count Széchényi ; " John Brahms with four volumes of Hungarian dances, Hungarian and Gipsy songs ; Raff with Hungarian dances ; Hofmann with a Hungarian suite ; Bülow a " Heroic March ; " Massenet, Hungarian March ; Delibes, parts of his ballet " Copélia ; " Mascagni, " Friend Fritz." Besides these the famous pianoforte and violin artists Dreischock, Thalberg, Wilmers, Schulhof, Rubinstein, Molique, Sarasate have written for their instruments Variations and Fantasias in Hungarian style with the introduction of favourite songs. When in 1860 operettas came into fashion some composers tried their powers in this branch. Among the earlier ones were

D

Géza Allaga and Charles Huber; afterwards Julius Káldy, Alexius Erkel, Béla Hegyi, Eugene Stojanovitcs.

More recently some have gained success in ballet music, and excellent music has been written by Charles Szabados, who with his ballet, " Viora," roused great enthusiasm. Eugene Stojanovitcs with his ballet " Csárdás," Stephen Kerner with " Le cheval de bronze," Lewis Tóth and Albert Metz with their ballet " Day and Night," have shown excellent powers of composition.

Many conspicuous countrymen of ours have won honour for Hungary abroad, *e.g.*, Josef Joachim, the greatest violinist of modern times, the Director of the High School in Berlin. Also among his compositions the most valuable is the Hungarian Concerto. Edward Reményi, Leopold Auer, Director of the Conservatorium at St. Petersburg, Edmund Singer, Rafael Josephi. Renowned conductors are Hans Richter, Sucher (Berlin), Seidel

(New York); singers: Mme. Mainville, Mme. Schoedel, Louise Liebhardt, Cornelia Hollósy, Rosa Csillag, Ida Benza, Francis Steger, Josef Wurda, John Beck, Lewis Bignio, etc.

As pianists and teachers we must further mention Antonio Sipos, with his numerous compositions for the piano, John Theindl and Willy Deutsch, who took an active part in the musical life of the capital. Teachers of composition were Michael Mosonyi and Alexander Nikolits; one might almost say that nearly all the younger generation have had their education from them. As writers on music beside the above mentioned Abrányi, are Gabriel Mátray and Stephen Bartalus. The first made the old Hungarian music known by his work "The melodies of historical, biblical and satirical Hungarian songs of the 17th century." Bartalus issued his interesting publication, "The Hungarian Orpheus," a collection of miscellaneous matter of the 18th and 19th centuries and a general collection of Hungarian songs.

Recently Julius Káldy with his works, "The Treasures of old Hungarian Music," "Old Hungarian War Songs," "Recruiting Songs," "Songs and Marches of the War for Freedom," has aroused much enthusiasm.

We must mention that in Hungary since the beginning of this century many institutions and schools for the cultivation of music have arisen. In Kolozsvár in 1819, the first Hungarian Conservatorium now existing was founded (the first Hungarian Opera was performed there in 1821). In 1833 Arad followed this example. An artistic association founded a similar institution at Pesth called The Musicians Society, which in its turn founded the National Conservatoire. In 1860, Debreczen founded in its turn a Conservatoire, while Kassa, Szeged and Sabadka, followed its example.

In 1860 the National Dramatic School

was opened in Budapest, in which operatic song was also taught. At the same time the Society of Musical Amateurs was founded, and the Musical Academy of Buda. Later in both these institutes a Music School was organized. In 1875 the National Hungarian Academy of Music was opened with Franz Liszt and Francis Erkel at the head of it. Ultimately the Hungarian School of Music was opened under the presidency of Julius Káldy, Alexander Nikolits and Julius Major, who have undertaken the special field of cultivation and instruction in Hungarian music.

Beside these there are in Budapest, as in the larger provincial towns, many musical and choral societies, and at Budapest as brilliant a concert season as at Vienna or Leipzig. In the first rank we must name the concerts of the Philharmonic Society, the Budapest Society of amateurs, the Buda Musical Academy, also the performances of the National

Academy of Music, the National and the Hungarian School of Music, and also the concerts of the several musical societies. We must add the appearance of many famous foreign violinists, pianists and singers who visit Budapest regularly.

Lately historical concerts have been started, by Stephen Bartalus and Julius Káldy reviving the most precious relics of the 17th and 18th centuries. These concerts, in consequence of their historical and scientific character, are generally given in the Hungarian Academy of Sciences.

We have cause for pride that Hungarian music has in a comparatively short time reached so high a level. If we compare it with the music of other nations the Italian, French, and German, the result is really surprising. At the Festivities of the thousandth year of the nation we can point to world-renowned composers among our countrymen and eminent works in all branches of music,

and having regard to the past development and advance of Hungarian music we
can look with full confidence and with
great hope to the future.

W. REEVES

AND

REEVES & TURNER'S.

Publications

CATALOGUE

OF WORKS

Literary . . .

Art and . . .

Music.

ALSO . . . .

Books on . . .

Freemasonry.

◇

London :

83, Charing Cross Rd.

W.C

PIANO TEACHING. Advice to Pupils and Young Teachers, by F. Le Couppey (Prof. in the Conservatory of Paris, etc.), Translated from the 3rd French Edition by M. A. Bierstadt, post 8vo, cloth, 2s.

A DESCRIPTION OF THE GREGORIAN TONES OR MODES AND THEIR VARIOUS ENDINGS, by John Hiles, post 8vo, 4d.

INTERLUDES. Seven Lectures, Collected and Edited by Stewart Macpherson, with Portrait, cr. 8vo, cloth, 2s. (pub. at 5s.)

MUSICAL ANALYSIS. A Handbook for Students, with Musical Illustrations, by H. C. Banister, crown 8vo, limp cloth, 2s.

ORGAN MUSIC.
(All with ped. obb.) (Prices Music—net).

Chopin's Nocturne (Op. 9, No. 2)	1s. 6d.	E. H. Lemare
Forward! Grand March . . .	1s. 6d.	E. H. Sugg
Lebanon March, The, (Smallwood)	2s.	Dr. Westbrook
Grand Festival March, " Illogan ".	2s.	
(also arr. for Piano Solo, and Vn. and Pf.)		H. C. Tonking
Overture to William Tell (Rossini),	2s. 6d.	A. Whittingham
Overture to Oberon (Weber). . .	2s.	A. Whittingham
Overture to Freischutz (Weber) .	2s.	A. Whittingham
Six Pieces for Church Use (arranged),	1s.	W. Smallwood

Now Ready.   Quarto cloth.   Price 7/6.

Modern Orchestral Instruments

Their Origin, Construction, and Use.

BEING A PRACTICAL ILLUSTRATED HAND-BOOK
For the use of
AMATEURS OR STUDENTS,
With many additional Illustrations, Tables, an . . . . .
. . . . Appendix, and an Explanatory Index.
BY
SCHLESINGER.

PREFACE.

THIS work owes its origin to a great want which has been felt by amateurs who wished to know something about the orchestra, and yet could find no practical book in English conveying the necessary information about the various instruments, *accompanied in each case by an illustration,* which should enable them to identify each one. Written to supply this want, it was advisable not to weary the reader with too many technicalities, while omitting no essential point.

Finally, I wish to express my gratitude to the many who have, by their generous help and advice as well as their just criticism, encouraged me in my work, and enabled me to complete it, and more especially to Mr. A. J. Hipkins, Mr. R. J. White, Mr. H. Grice, Mr. Algernon Rose, Mr. George Morley, Mr. Arthur Hill Mr. Klussmann, Mr. A. C. White, and Mr. Schulz-Curtius; to Miss Mabel Goschen, to whom I am indebted for help in compiling the index; also to those who have kindly lent me blocks or photographs for the purpose of illustration, and whose names will be found in a separate list.

THE LARGE EDITION, over 1,000 pp., imp. 8vo.

CHAFFERS (Wm.), MARKS AND MONOGRAMS ON
EUROPEAN AND ORIENTAL POTTERY AND
PORCELAIN, with Historical Notices of each Manu-
factory, preceded by an Introductory Essay on An-
cient Pottery and on the Vasa Fictilia ot England and
Mediæval Earthenware Vessels, with over 3,500 Potters
Marks and Illustrations, revised and edited by F.
Litchfield, ornamental cloth, Ninth Edition, with Ad-
ditional Information and Marks, 42s.

New Edition in Hand.

CHAFFERS (W.), HALL MARKS ON GOLD AND
SILVER PLATE, Illustrated with Revised Tables of
Annual Date Letters employed in the Assay Offices
of the United Kingdom, roy. 8vo, cloth.

This edition contains a History of the Goldsmith's Trade in France, with
extracts from the decrees relating thereto, and engravings of the standard
and other Marks used in that country as well as in other foreign States.
The Provincial Tables of England and Scotland contain many hitherto unpublished Marks ; all the recent enactments are quoted The London Tables
(which have never been surpassed for correctness) may now be considered
complete Many valuable Hints to Collectors are given, and cases of fraud
alluded to, etc.

THE COMPANION TO "HALL MARKS ON GOLD AND SILVER
PLATE."

CHAFFERS (W.), GILDA AURIFABRORUM, A History
of English Goldsmiths and Plateworkers and their
Marks stamped on Plate, copied in *facsimile* from
celebrated Examples and the earliest Records preserved at Goldsmiths' Hall, London, with their names,
addresses and dates ot entry, 2.500 *Illustrations;* also
Historical Account of the Goldsmiths' Company and
their Hall Marks and Regalia ; the Mint ; Closing of
the Exchequer ; Goldsmith Bankers : Shop Signs, a
Copious Index, etc., a New Edition, 267 pp., roy. 8vo,
cloth, 12s.

CHAFFERS (W.), COLLECTOR'S HANDBOOK OF
MARKS AND MONOGRAMS ON POTTERY AND
PORCELAIN OF THE RENAISSANCE AND MOD-
ERN PERIOD, selected from his larger work, New
Edition Revised and considerably Augmented by F.
Litchfield, Twelfth Thousand, 234 pp., post 8vo, cloth,
gilt, 6s.

CHAFFERS (Wm.) HANDBOOK TO HALL MARKS ON GOLD AND SILVER PLATE, with Revised Tables of Annual Date Letters Employed in the Assay Offices of England, Scotland and Ireland, Extended by C. A. Markham, *F.S.A.*, cr. 8vo, cloth, 5s.   1902

MARKHAM (Chr. A., *F.S.A.*) HANDBOOK TO FOREIGN HALL MARKS ON GOLD AND SILVER PLATE (except those on French Plate), containing 163 stamps, cr. 8vo, cloth, 5s.

MARKHAM (C.). HANDBOOK TO FRENCH HALL MARKS ON GOLD AND SILVER PLATE. Illustrated. Crown 8vo, cloth, 5s.   1900

COBBETT (W.), RURAL RIDES in the Counties of Surrey, Kent, Sussex, Hants., Wilts., Gloucestershire, etc., edited with Life, New Notes, and the addition of a copious Index, New Edition by PITT COBBETT, *map and portrait*, 2 vols, cr. 8vo, (xlviii. and 806 pp.), cloth gilt, 12s. 6d.

Cobbett's "Rural Rides" is to us a delightful book, but it is one which few people know. We are not sure that up to the present time it was impossible to get a nice edition of it. We are therefore glad to see that Messrs· Reeves & Turner's recently published edition is a very creditable production two handy well-filled volumes.—*Gardening*

KEATS (John), THE POETICAL WORKS OF JOHN KEATS (large type), given from his own Editions and other Authentic Sources, and collated with many Manuscripts, edited by H. Buxton Forman, *portrait*, SEVENTH EDITION, 8 pp., cr. 8vo, buckram, 7s. 6d. 1902

THE LETTERS OF JOHN KEATS (Large type), Complete Revised Edition, with a Portrait not published in previous Editions, and 24 Contemporary Views of Places visited by Keats, Edited by H. Buxton Forman, 519 pp., cr. 8vo, buckram, 8s.

THE AWAKENING OF WOMEN; or Woman's Part in Evolution, by Francis Swiney, crown 8vo, cloth, 5s. *net.*

"Strong and soul-stirring. . . . . . The book of the age on the woman question."—*The Woman's Tribune.*
It is most carefully thought out. . . . . . The authorities quoted all seem to point to the fact that woman is more highly evolved than man.—*Mrs. Ada Ballin, editor of* "WOMANHOOD"

SHELLEY'S PRINCIPLES has time refuted or confirmed them, a Retrospect and Forecast, by H. S. Salt, post 8vo, 1s.

PERCY BYSSHE SHELLEY, Poet and Pioneer, a Biographical Study by H. S. Salt, etched portrait, cr. 8vo, cloth, 3s. 6d.

SHELLEY LIBRARY (The), An Essay in Bibliography, by H. Buxton Forman, Shelley's Books, Pamphlets and Broadsides, Posthumous Separate Issues, and Posthumous Books, wholly or mainly by him, 127 pp,, 8vo, parts 1 and 2, wrappers, 3s. 6d. each.

A SHELLEY PRIMER, By H. S. Salt, cr. 8vo, bds. 2s. 6d.

SHELLEY (Percy Bysshe), THE POETICAL WORKS (in large type), given from his own Editions and other Authentic Sources, collated with many MSS., and with all Editions of Authority, together with his Prefaces and Notes, his Poetical Translations and Fragments, and an Appendix of Juvenalia, Edited by H. Buxton Forman, with the Notes of Mary Wollstonecraft Shelley, *fine etched portrait*, 2 vols., cr. 8vo, cloth (with Design in Gold on cover by Rossetti), 12s. *Fourth Edition in the press.*

SIDONIA THE SORCERESS, by William Meinhold. Translated by Lady Wilde, with the Amber Witch, translated by Lady Duff Gordon, in 2 vols., crown 8vo, 8s. 6d.   1894

THOMSON (James, "B. V."), POETICAL WORKS, The City of Dreadful Night, Vane's Story, Weddah and Om-el-Bonain, Voice from the Hell, and Poetical Remains, Edited by B. Dobell, with Memoir and Portrait, 2 vols, thick cr. 8vo, cloth, 12s. 6d.

THOMSON (James. "B. V."), BIOGRAPHICAL AND CRITICAL STUDIES, 483 pages, cr. 8vo, cloth, **6s.**

Dedicated by permission to Sir Henry Irving.
ALFRED THE GREAT (a Drama). The Ballad of Dundee and other Poems, by Florence G. Attenborough. Cr. 8vo, cloth, 3s. 6d.

THE CHILD : ITS ORIGIN AND DEVELOPMENT. A Manual enabling Mothers to Initiate their Daughters gradually and modestly into all the Mysteries of Life, by Dora Langlois, cr. 8vo, sewed, 1s.

A CREED FOR CHRISTIAN SOCIALISTS, with Expositions by Charles William Stubbs, D.D. (The Dean of Ely). Cr. 8vo, cloth, 2s. (paper, 1s.)

COMTE (Auguste), General View of Positivism, translated by J. H. Bridges. 2nd Edition, cr. 8vo, cloth, 2s. 6d.

THE SOCIAL ASPECTS OF CHRISTIANITY, and other Essays by Richard T. Ely, Ph.D. Cr. 8vo, cloth, 2s. (paper, 1s.)

PROGRESS AND POVERTY, by Henry George. Cloth, 1s. 6d., or Cabinet Edition, cloth, 2s. 6d. (paper, 1s.)

KARL MARX'S THEORY OF VALUE (Complete), forming the First 9 Chapters of " Capital." Cr. 8vo, cloth, 2s. (paper, 1s.)

LOOKING BACKWARD, by Edward Bellamy, with copious Index and Portrait. Limp cloth, 1s. 6d., Cabinet Edition, Steel Portrait, 2s. 6d. (also cheap editions, paper covers. 6d. and 1s.)

CO-OPERATIVE COMMONWEALTH : Exposition of Modern Socialism, by L. Gronlund. English Edition. Third Edition. Edited by B. Shaw. Cr. 8vo, cloth, 2s. (paper, 1s.)

TENNYSON AS A THINKER, by Henry S. Salt, paper, 6d. (or large paper copies, 1s. 6d.)

PATRIOTISM AND CHRISTIANITY, by Count Leo Tolstoy. Cr. 8vo, cloth, 1s. (paper, 6d.)

LAWS OF ETERNAL LIFE : Being Studies in the Church Catechism by Rev. Stewart D. Headlam. Cr. 8vo, cloth, 2s. (paper, 1s.)

WOMAN. Her Position in the Past, Present and Future, by August Bebel. cr. 8vo, cloth. 2s.

WHAT IS PROPERTY? An Inquiry into the Principle of Right and of Government, by P. J. PROUDHON, Translated by B. R. TUCKER, crown 8vo, cloth, 3s. 6d.

HISTORICAL, BIOGRAPHICAL WORKS, &c.

MAKERS OF MUSIC, Biographical Sketches of the Great Composers, With Chronological Summaries of their Works, and Facsimiles from Musical MSS. of Bach, Handel, Purcell, Dr. Arne, Gluck, Haydn, Mozart, Beethoven, Weber, Schubert, Berlioz, Mendelssohn, Chopin, Schu nann, Wagner, Verdi, Gounod, Brahms and Grieg, with General Chronological Table. By R. Far-quharson Sharp, Portrait of Purcell, *Second Edition*, cr. 8vo, cloth, 5s.

HOW TO MANAGE A CHORAL SOCIETY. By N. Kilburn, 2nd Edition, post 8vo., 6d.

WAGNER'S PARSIFAL and the Bayreuth Fest-Spielhaus. By N. Kilburn, cr. 8vo., 6d.

WAGNER, A Sketch of his Life and Works, by N. Kilburn, 6d.

WOMAN AS A MUSICIAN, an art Historical Study by F. R. Ritter, 8vo., 1s.

ÆSTHETICS OF MUSICAL ART, or the Beautiful in Music by Dr. F. Hand, translated by W. E. Lawson, Mus. Bac., cr. 8vo., cloth, 5s.

EHLERT (LOUIS), Letters on Music to a Lady, translated by F. Raymond Ritter, cr. 8vo., bevelled cloth, gilt edges, 4s. 6d., plain cloth, 4s.

CHERUBINI, Memorials illustrative of his Life, by E. Bellasis, thick crown 8vo, cloth, 6s.

BERLIOZ, LIFE AND LETTERS, from the French by H. M. Dunstan, 2 vols., cr. 8vo., cloth, 10s. 6d. (pub. 21s.)

THE BACH LETTERS. Letters of Samuel Wesley, relating to the Introduction into England of the Works of Bach. Ed. by E. Wesley. 2nd Edition, 8vo. cl., 2s. 6d.

MEZZOTINTS IN MODERN MUSIC, Brahms, Tchaïkovsky, Chopin, Strauss, Liszt, and Wagner, By Jas. Huneker, cr. 8vo, cloth, gilt top, 7s. 6d.

SKETCHES OF ENGLISH GLEE COMPOSERS, Historical, Biographical and Critical (From about 1735-1866), by D. Baptie, post 8vo, cloth, 5s.

LIFE OF ROBERT SCHUMANN, with Letters, 1833-1852, by von Wasielewski, Translated by A. L. Alger, with Preface by W. A. Barrett, B. Mus. cr. 8vo, cloth, 8s. 6d.

FRANZ LISZT, by T. Carlaw Martin, 6d.

HALF A CENTURY OF MUSIC IN ENGLAND, 1837-1887, By F. Hueffer, 8vo, cloth, 3s. 6d. (pub. 8s. 6d.)

TEMPLETON AND MALIBRAN : Reminiscences of these Renowned Singers, with Original Letters and Anecdotes, 3 Authentic Portraits by Mayall, 8vo, cloth, 2s. 6d.

BALFE, His Life and Works, by W. A. Barrett, er. 8vo, bevelled cloth, 3s. 6d. (pub. 7s. 6d.)

STATHAM (H. H.), Form and Design in Music, a Brief Outline of the Æsthetic conditions of the Art, addressed to general Readers (in a readable Literary form . . . in everyday language), 8vo, cloth, 2s. (pub. 5s.)

BEETHOVEN, by Richard Wagner, with a Supplement from the Philosophical Works of Arthur Schopenhauer, trans. by Edward Dannreuther, 2nd Ed., cr. 8vo, cl., 6s.

CHOPIN, LIFE OF, by Franz Liszt, new and very much Enlarged Edition, Englished in full now for the first time by John Broadhouse, cr. 8vo, cloth, 6s.

WAGNER, Der Ring des Nibelungen, being the story concisely told of Das Rhinegold, Die Walküre, Siegfried and Götterdämmerung, by N. Kilburn, post 8vo, 9d.

Box (C.), Church Music in the Metropolis, its Past and present Condition, with Notes Critical and Explanatory, post 8vo, cloth, 3s.

THE PAST AND THE FUTURE, INAUGURAL LECTURE AT GRESHAM COLLEGE, Nov. 1890, by J. Frederick Bridge Mus. Doc., cr. 8vo, sewed, 6d.

ENGLISH HYMN TUNES from the 16th Century to the Present Time, by the Rev. A. W. Malim, containing 21 Musical Illustrations, 8vo, sewed, 1s.

BEETHOVEN, Life of, by Louis Nohl, translated by John J. Lalor, 2nd Edition, cr. 8vo, bevelled cloth, gilt edges, 3s. 6d.

ENGLISH GLEE AND MADRIGAL WRITERS, by W. A. Barrett, 8vo, cloth, 2s. 6d.

BEETHOVEN DEPICTED BY HIS CONTEMPORARIES, by Ludwig Nohl, translated by E. Hill, 2nd Edition, thick cr. 8vo, cloth, 7s. 6d.

|EDUCATIONAL.|

DICTIONARY OF MUSICIANS, (Cocks') New and Enlarged Edition brought completely up to date, post 8vo, sewed, 1s., cloth, 1s. 6d.

MUSIC, A First Book for Beginners embodying the most recent English and Continental Teaching by a Professor [Alfred Whittingham], post 8vo, 4d.
The two principal objects kept in view in writing this little book were Thoroughness of Definition and Regular Order in the arrangement of Subjects. It differs from all other similar Works in that all the Technical Terms in Music are introduced in the Answers not in the Questions.

COUNTERPOINT : A Simple and Intelligible Treatise, Containing the most Important Rules of all Text Books, in Catechetical Form ; (Forming an Answer to the Question " What is Counterpoint ? ") Intended for Beginners. By A. Livingstone Hirst, cr. 8vo, sewed, 9d.

MANUAL OF MUSICAL HISTORY, from the Epoch of Ancient Greece to our present time by Dr. F. L. Ritter' 2nd Edition, cr. 8vo, cl., 2s. 6d.

ON CONDUCTING, by Richard Wagner, translated by E. Dannreuther, Second Edition, cr. 8vo., cloth, 5s.

MUSIC IN ENGLAND, by Dr. F. L. Ritter, cr. 8vo, cl., 6s.

MUSIC IN AMERICA, by Dr. F. L. Ritter, cr. 8vo, bevelled cloth, 7s. 6d.

DUDLEY BUCK'S Complete Pronouncing Dictionary of Musical Terms. By Dr. Dudley Buck. *Third Edition with the Pronunciation of each Term accurately given,* cr. 8vo, paper cover 6d., (cloth 1s).

THE STUDENT'S HELMHOLTZ, Musical Acoustics or the Phenomena of Sound as connected with Music, by John Broadhouse, with more than 100 Illustrations, 3rd Edition, cr. 8vo, cloth, 7s. 6d.

THE STUDENT'S HISTORY OF MUSIC. History f Music, from the Christian Era to the present time by Dr. F. L. Ritter. 3rd Edition, thick cr. 8vo., cloth, 7s. 6d.

HARMONY AND THE CLASSIFICATION OF CHORDS, with Questions and Exercises, by Dr. J. H. Lewis, Vol. 1, 8vo, boards, cloth back, 5s.

ELEMENTARY MUSIC. A book for Beginners, by Dr. Westbrook, with Questions and Vocal Exercises, Thirteenth Edition, 1s., (cloth, 1s. 6d).

PURITY IN MUSIC, by A. F. Thibaut. Translated by J. Broadhouse. Schumann says: "A fine book about music, read it frequently." Crown 8vo., cloth, 2s. 6d.

LIFE AND WORKS OF HANDEL. By A. Whittingham. 1s. (cloth, 1s. 6d.)

LIFE AND WORKS OF MOZART. By A. Whittingham. 1s. (cloth, 1s. 6d.)

EXERCISES ON GENERAL ELEMENTARY MUSIC. A Book for Beginners, by K. Paige, 4th Edition, Part I. price 9d., Part II. price 1s.(2 parts complete in cloth, 2/4
The *Musical Times* speaks in the highest terms of this work.

DR. AHN'S FIRST FRENCH COURSE. Edited by S. Bartlett (Head Master Mercers' and Stationers' School), Post 8vo., cloth, 1s. 6d.

THE HARMONISING OF MELODIES, A Text-Book for Students and Beginners, by H. C. Banister, cr. 8vo, 2s.

MUSICAL SHORTHAND for Composers, Students of Harmony, Counterpoint, etc., can be written very rapidly and is more legible than printed music, with Specimens from Bach, Handel, Chopin, Wagner, Mendelssohn, Spohr, Mozart, etc., by Francis Taylor, 14 pages, 12mo, 6d.
"Composers and Students of Music expend a vast amount of time in mere painful mechanism." We have only six totally unlike signs. These from their simplicity can be written with great rapidity, one dip of the pen sufficing for an entire page, and the writing being as legible as possible.—*Preface.*

| WORKS ON THE PIANOFORTE, &c. |

GREATER WORKS OF CHOPIN, (Polonaises, Mazurkas, Nocturnes, etc.) and how they should be played, by J. Kleczynski, translated by Miss N. Janotha and edited by Sutherland Edwards, with Portrait, Facsimile, etc., cr. 8vo, cloth, 5s.

MUSIC AND MUSICIANS, Essays and Criticisms, by Robert Schumann, translated, edited and annotated by F. R. Ritter, Portrait of Robert Schumann, photographed from a Crayon by Bendemann, First Series, *Sixth Edition*, thick cr. 8vo, cloth, 8s. 6d.

Ditto, 2nd Series, 2nd Edition, thick cr. 8vo, cl.,10s. 6d.

EHRENFECHTER (C. A.), Technical Study in the art o, Pianoforte Playing (Deppe's principles), with numerous illustrations, fourth edition, cr. 8vo, bevelled cl., 2s. 6d.

AN ESSAY ON THE THEORY AND PRACTICE OF TUNING IN GENERAL, and on Schiebler's Invention of Tuning Pianofortes and Organs by the Metronome in Particular, Trans. by A. Wehrhan, sewed, 1s.

THE ART OF MODULATION, A Hand-book Showing at a Glance the Modulations from one Key to any other on the Octave, etc., Edited by Carli Zoeller, 2nd Edition, roy. 8vo, paper, 2s. 6d. or cloth, 4s.

EHRENFECHTER (C. A.), Delivery in the Art of Piano-forte Playing, on Rhythm, Measure, Phrasing, Tempo, cr. 8vo, cloth, 2s.

BEETHOVEN'S PIANOFORTE SONATAS Explained by Ernst von Elterlein trans. by E. Hill, with Preface by Ernst Pauer, entirely new and revised edition (the Fifth), with Portrait, Facsimile and View of House, cr. 8vo, cloth, 3s. 6d.

BEETHOVEN'S SYMPHONIES in their Ideal Significance, explained by Ernst von Elterlein, translated by Francis Weber, with an account of the facts relating to Beethoven's 10th Symphony, by L. Nohl, *Second Edition*, with Portrait, cr. 8vo, cloth, 3s. 6d.

BEETHOVEN'S SYMPHONIES Critically discussed by A. T. Teetgen. *Second Edition*, cloth, 3s. 6d.

THE DEPPE FINGER EXERCISES for rapidly developing an Artistic Touch in Pianoforte Playing, carefully arranged, classified and explained by Amy Fay, English Fingering, folio, 1s. 6d. (Continental Fingering, 1s. 6d.)

HOW TO PLAY CHOPIN. The Works of Chopin and their proper Interpretation. By KLECZYNSKI, translated by A. WHITTINGHAM, 5th. Ed., *Woodcut and Music Illus.* Post 8vo, cloth, 3s. 6d.

SCHUMANN'S RULES AND MAXIMS for young Musicians. 4d.

PRACTICE REGISTER for Pupil's Daily Practice. A specimen, 1d., or 1s. 4d. per 100.

REEVES' VAMPING TUTOR, Art of Extemporaneous Accompaniment or Playing by ear on the Pianoforte rapidly enabling anyone having an ear for music (with or without any knowledge of musical notation), to

accompany Waltzes, Polkas, Songs, and with equal
facility in any key, with practical examples, including
Ma Normandi (in C), Lilla's a Lady, The Swiss Boy,
Home, Sweet Home, Blue Bells of Scotland, Nancy
Dawson, Ma Normandi (in A), The Miller of the Dea
by Francis Taylor, folio, 2s.

The Great Classic for the Piano.

BACH (J. S.), 48 Preludes and 48 Fugues in all the
major and minor keys in 2 vols, folio, 3s. each (or in 1
vol, stiff covers, cloth back, 7s. 6d.

MOZART'S Don Giovanni, a Commentary, from the
3rd French Edition of Charles Gounod, by W. Clark
and J. T. Hutchinson, cr. 8vo, cloth, 3s. 6d.

TUNING THE PIANOFORTE.—SMITH (Hermann), The
Art of Tuning the Pianoforte, a New and Comprehen-
sive Treatise to enable the musician to Tune his Pf.
upon the System founded on the Theory of Equal Tem-
perament, cr. 8vo, limp cloth, *New Ed. thoroughly
revised*, 2s.

A HISTORY OF PIANOFORTE MUSIC, With Critical
Estimates of its Greatest Masters and Sketches of
their Lives, by John C. Fillmore, cr. 8vo, cloth, 3s. 6d.

TRANSPOSITION AT SIGHT, For Students of the Organ
and Pianoforte, by H. Ernst Nichol, 2nd Edition, cr.
8vo, sewed, 1s., cloth, 1s. 6d.

THE VIOLIN.

INFORMATION FOR PLAYERS, OWNERS, DEALERS AND
MAKERS OF BOW INSTRUMENTS, ALSO FOR STRING MANU-
FACTURERS, taken from Personal Experiences, Studies
and Observations, by William Hepworth, with Illustrations of Stainer and Guarnerius Violins, etc., cr. 8vo,
cloth, 2s. 6d.

NOTICE OF ANTHONY STRADIVARI, the celebrated Violin Maker known by the name of Stradivarius, preceded
by Historical and Critical Researches on the Origin and
Transformations of Bow Instruments, and followed by a
Theoretical Analysis of the Bow, etc., by F. J. Fetis,
translated by J. Bishop, Facsimile, 8vo, cloth, 5s.

BIOGRAPHICAL DICTIONARY OF FIDDLERS, including
Performers on the Violoncello and Double Bass, Past
and Present, containing a Sketch of their Artistic
Career, together with Notes of their Compositions, by A.
Mason Clarke, with 9 portraits, post 8vo, bevelled cl., 5s.

How to Make a Violin, Practically Treated, 2 Folding Plates and many Illustrations, by J. Broadhouse, cr. 8vo, bevelled cloth, 3s. 6d.

Violin Manufacture in Italy and its German Origin, by Dr. E. Schebek, translated by W. E. Lawson, 8vo., sewed, 1s.

Sketches of Great Violinists and Great Pianists, Biographical and Anecdotal, with Account of the Violin and Early Violinists (Viotti, Spohr, Paganini, De Beriot, Ole Bull, Clementi, Moscheles, Schumann (Robert and Clara), Chopin, Thalberg, Gottschalk, Liszt), by G. T. Ferris ; Second Edition, bevelled cloth, 3s 6d. (or gilt edges, 4s. 6d.)

Facts about Fiddles, Violins Old and New. By J. Broadhouse, 3rd Edition, 6d.

Technics of Violin Playing. By Karl Courvoisier. With Illustrations, 4th Edition, paper 1s. (or cloth, thick paper, 2s. 6d.) Highly commended by Joachim.

How to Play the Fiddle, for Beginners on the Violin. By H.W. and G.Gresswell. 4th edition, 1s.,(cl, 2s.)

Autobiography of Louis Spohr. 2 vols in 1, thick 8vo, cloth, 7s. 6d. (pub. 15s.)

Treatise on the Structure and Preservation of the Violin and all other Bow Instruments, together with an account of the most celebrated makers and of the genuine characteristics of their Instruments, by J. A. Otto, with additions by J. Bishop, cr. 8vo, cloth, 3s.

ORGAN WORKS.

Analysis of Mendelssohn's Organ Works, a Study of their Structural Features, for the use of Students, 127 Musical Examples, portrait and facsimiles, cr. 8vo, bevelled cloth, 4s. 6d.

Organist's Quarterly Journal of Original Compositions. Edited by Dr. W. Spark, non-subscribers, 5s. net, per part. For Contents see end of Catalogue.

New Series Volume, 160 large pages, oblong folio, bound in cloth, 18s.

Rink's Practical Organ School : A New Edition, Carefully Revised. The Pedal Part printed on a separate Staff, and the Preface, Remarks and Technical Terms translated from the German, expressly for this, edition by John Hiles. The Six Books Complete, handsomely bound in red cloth, gilt edges, ob, folio, 10s. 6d. (issued at 20s.), or the six parts 7s. 6d. (issued at 6s. each.)

ORGANS AND ORGANISTS IN PARISH CHURCHES, A Handbook of the Law relating to the Custody, Control and Use of Organs, and to the Position, Lights, and Disabilities of Organists, to which is Added a Chapter on the Hiring of Pianos, and on "The Three Years System," by William C. A. Blow, M.A., Oxon., of the Inner Temple, Esq., Barrister-at-Law, cr. 8vo, cl., 2s. 6d.

A SHORT HISTORY OF THE ORGAN, Organists, and Services of the Chapel of Alleyn's College, Dulwich, with Extracts from the Diary of the Founder, by W. H. Stocks, cr. 8vo, sewed, 1s.

THE INFLUENCE OF THE ORGAN IN HISTORY. By Dudley Buck, 1s.

HENRY SMART'S ORGAN COMPOSITIONS Analysed. By J. Broadhouse, cr. 8vo, cloth, 2s. 6d.

REFORM IN ORGAN BUILDING, by Thomas Casson, 6d.

THE ORGAN, Its Compass, Tablature, and Short and Incomplete Octaves, by John W. Warman, A.C.O., imp. 8vo, sewed, 3s. 6d. or boards, cloth back, 4s. 6d.

CATECHISM for the Harmonium and American Organ, by John Hiles, post 8vo, sewed, 1s.

RIMBAULT (Dr. E. F.), The Early English Organ Builders and their Works, from the 15th Century to the Period of the Great Rebellion, an unwritten chapter on the History of the Organ, Well printed, with woodcuts, post 8vo, cloth, 3s. 6d.

| VOICE AND SINGING |

TWELVE LESSONS ON BREATHING AND BREATH CONTROL, for Singers, Speakers and Teachers, by Geo. E. Thorp, crown 8vo, limp cloth, 1s.

TWENTY LESSONS ON THE DEVELOPMENT OF THE VOICE, or Singers Speakers and Teachers, by Geo. E. Thorp, crown 8vo, limp cloth, 1s.

50 MUSICAL HINTS TO CLERGYMEN, Management of Breath, Classification of Male Voices, Management of the Voice, The Service, with twenty specially written Exercises by Geo. F. Grover, 1s.

CATECHISM OF PART SINGING AND THE CHORAL SERvices. By John Hiles, 3rd Edition, thick post 8vo, price 1s.
Advice to Singers on every point of interest in reference to the Vocal Organs

THE THROAT IN ITS RELATION TO SINGING, a series of Popular Papers by Whitfield Ward, A.M., M.D. *With engravings*, cloth, 3s. 6d.

HOW TO SING AN ENGLISH BALLAD. By E. Philp, 7th Edition, 6d.

VOCAL EXERCISES FOR CHOIRS AND SCHOOLS. By Dr· Westbrook, 2d.

RUDIMENTS OF VOCAL MUSIC. With 42 Preparatory Exercises, Rounds and Songs in the Treble Clef, by T. Mee Pattison, 2nd Ed., 4d.

SOME FAMOUS SONGS, an Art Historical Sketch. By F. R. Ritter. 1s.

VOICE PRODUCTION AND VOWEL ENUNCIATION, by F. F. Mewburn Levien, Diagrams by Arthur C. Behrend, post 8vo, 6d.

POSITION AND ACTION IN SINGING, a Study of the True Conditions of Tone, a Solution of Automatic (Artistic) Breath Control, by Edmund J. Myer, cr. 8vo, 4s. 6d.

NATIONAL SCHOOL OF OPERA IN ENGLAND ; being The Substance of a Paper read before the Licentiates of Trinity College, March, 1882, by Frank Austin, post 8vo, sewed, 6d.

MISCELLANEOUS

LORD CHESTERFIELD'S LETTERS TO HIS SON.—Edited with Occasional Elucidatory Notes, Translations of all the Latin, French and Italian Quotations, and a Biographical Notice of the Author. By Chas. Stokes Carey, 2 vols, cr. 8vo, bevelled cloth, 10s. 6d.

FLAGELLATION AND THE FLAGELLANTS, A History of the Rod, in all Countries by the Rev. W. M. Cooper, *Plates and Cuts*, thick cr. 8vo, cloth, 7s. 6d. (pub. 12s. 6d.)

CLASSICAL WORKS.
Edited by Prof. Anthon.

ANTHON'S HORACE, Edited by Rev. James Boyd, LL.D., thick post 8vo, 5s. 6d.

ANTHON'S HOMER'S ILIAD, First Three Books, Edited by B. Davies, LL.D., thick post 8vo, 5s. 6d.

ANTHON'S CÆSAR'S COMMENTARIES, Edited by Rev. G. B. Wheeler, thick post 8vo, 4s. 6d.

ANTHON'S ECLOGUES AND GEORGICS OF VIRGIL, with English Notes, Critical and Explanatory, and a Metrical Index, post 8vo, price 4s. 6d.

ANTHON'S SALLUST, Edited by Rev. J. Boyd, L.L.D., post 8vo, 4s. 6d.

ANTHON'S JUVENAL AND PERSIUS' SATIRES, Edited by J. T. Wheeler, post 8vo, 4s. 6d.

ANTHON'S CICERO'S ORATIONS, with English Commentary and Historical, Geographical and Legal Indexes, Revised and Edited by Rev. G. B. Wheeler, post 8vo, 4s. 6d.

LIFE OF DAVID GARRICK, by J. Smyth, post 8vo, boards, 1s.

RUDIMENTS OF GREEK GRAMMAR, by E. Wettenhall, D.D., translated by Rev. G. N. Wright, numerous annotations and Questions for Examination, by Rev. G. B. Wheeler, 3s.

HOW TO UNDERSTAND WAGNER'S "RING OF THE NIBELUNG," being the Story and a Descriptive Analysis of the "Rheingold," the "Valkyr," "Siegfried" and the "Dusk of the Gods," with a number of Musical Examples by Gustave Kobbé, Sixth Edition, post 8vo cloth, 3s. 6d.

"To be appreciated in the smallest wa Wagner must   studied in advance."—*Illustrated London News.*

RATIONAL ACCOMPANIMENT TO THE PSALMS by F. Gilbert Webb, post 8vo, 6d.

HOW TO PLAY FROM SCORE.—Treatise on Accompaniment from Score on the Organ or Pianoforte, by F. J. Fetis, trans. by A. Whittingham, cr. 8vo, cloth 3s. 6d.

CHOIR LISTS FOR SUNDAY SERVICES.

No. 1. Morning and Evening, printed in red, 1s. 4d.
per 100.

No. 2. Morning, Afternoon, and Evening, printed in
red, 1s. 6d. per 100.

No. 3. Morning and Evening, printed in red and
black, 1s. 8d. per 100.

No. 4. Morning and Even., printed in red 1s. 6d.
per 100.

No. 5. Quarto Size, Matins, Litany, Holy Com-
munion, First Evensong, Second Evensong, Gothic
Letter, printed in red, 6d. per dozen, 3s. per 100.

CHOIR ATTENDANCE REGISTER, 8vo, cloth.

No. 1. Ruled for a Choir of 20 or less, for one year,
beginning at any date, 1s. 6d.

No. 2. Ruled for a Choir of 40 or less, or one year,
beginning at any date, 2s.

No. 3. Ruled for a choir of 60 or less, for one year,
beginning at any date, 2s. 6d.

Performing Edition.

THE CREATION, A Sacred Oratorio composed by
Joseph Haydn, Vocal Score, The Pianoforte Accompaniment arranged and the whole edited by G. A.
Macfarren, 8vo, paper covers, 2s., boards, 2s. 6d., scarlet
cloth, 4s.

SIXTY YEARS OF MUSIC : A Record of the Art in England during the Victorian Era, containing 70 Portrait.
of the most Eminent Musicians, oblong quarto, boards,
cloth back, 2s. 6d.

FROM LYRE TO MUSE, A History of the Aboriginal
Union of Music and Poetry, By J. Donovan, cr. 8vo,
cloth, 2s. 6d.

KING'S ROYAL ALBUMS, Nos. 1 and 2.
NATIONAL AND PATRIOTIC SONG ALBUM.
With Pf. Acc., containing the following popular pieces,
in 2 Bks., 1s. each.

BOOK 1.

God Save the King
God Bless the Prince of Wales
There's a Land (Dear Eng-
[land
Victoria
God Bless our Sailor Prince
Here's a Health unto His
[Majesty
Lord of the Sea
Roast Beef of Old England
The Blue Bells of Scotland
Tom Bowling
Come Lassies and Lads
Ye Mariners of England
The Bay of Biscay

BOOK 2.

Hearts of Oak
Stand United
The Cause of England's
Greatness
The Last Rose of Summer
The Leather Bottle
Home, Sweet Home
Three Cheers for the Red
White and Blue
The Minstrel Boy
The British Grenadiers
Auld Lang Syne
Rule Britannia

King's Royal Albums, No. 3.   Price 1/-
10 MARCHES FOR THE PIANO.   BY J. P. SOUSA.

1. The Washington Post.
2. Manhatton Beach.
3. The Liberty Bell.
4. High School Cadets.
5. The Belle of Chicago.
6. The Corcoran Cadets.

7. Our Flirtation.
8. March past of the Rifle
   Regiment.
9. March past of the
   National Fencibles.
10. Semper Fidelis.

King's Royal Album, No. 4.   Price 1/-
SIX ORGAN PIECES FOR CHURCH USE.
EDITED BY WILLIAM SMALLWOOD.
With Ped. Obb., Selections from rarely known works.

1. Moderato con moto
2. Adagio Expressivo
3. Andante Moderato

4. Andante Religioso
5. Andante con moto
6. Lento Cantabile

King's Royal Album, No. 5.   Price 1/-
SMALLWOOD'S ESMERALDA ALBUM FOR PIANO.

Belgium (Galop).
Belle of Madrid (Tempi di
Polka).
Emmeline (Galop).

Esmeralda (Transcription
on Levey's Popular Song).
Placid Stream (Morceau).
The Seasons (Galop).

King's Royal Album, No. 6.   Price 6d.
BALFE'S ROSE OF CASTILLE, 6 FAVOURITE MELODIES.
easily arranged for the Pianoforte by E. F. Rimbault.
1. Convent Cell (The).
2. 'Twas Rank and Fame.
3. Tho' fortune darkly o'er me frown.
4. I am a simple Muleteer.
5. I'm not the Queen.
6. List to the Gay Castanet.

POPULAR PART SONGS.
1. Merrily goes the Mill, by T. B. Southgate, 1d.
2. Take, O Take those Lips away, Part Song for S.A.T.B. by Claude E. Cover, A.R.C.O., 1½d.
3. Pack Clouds Away, for S.A.T.B., by Claude E. Cover, A.R.C.O., 2d.
4. Summer Roses, for S.A.T.B., by G. Rayleigh Vicars, 2d.
5. Erin, Dear Erin, for T.A.T.B., by Churchill Sibley, 2d.

MODERN CHURCH MUSIC.
1. Easter Anthem, "Jesus Lives!" by Rev. T. Herbert Spinney, price 2d.
2. Anthem for Whitsuntide and General Use, "Come Holy Ghost our Souls Inspire," by Thomas Adams, F.R.C.O., price 2d.
3. Story of the Ascension, by Rev. John Napleton, price 1½d.
4. Anthem, "God so Loved the World," by J. Jamouneau, price 2d.
5. Magnificat in B flat, by Thomas Adams, F.R.C.O., Price 3d.
6. Nunc Dimittis in B flat, by Thomas Adams, F.R.C.O., Price 2d.
7. Four Kyries, by Charles Steggall, Berthold Tours, E. J. Hopkins, J. M. W. Young, price 1½d.
8. Te Deum, by T. E. Spinney, 1½d.
9. Anthem, "I am the Good Shepherd," by G. Rayleigh Vicars, 2d.
10. Story of the Cross, Music by H. Clifton Bowker, 2d.
12. Story of the Cross, Music by Dr. Geo. Prior, 2d.

THE ORGANIST'S QUARTERLY JOURNAL.

Of Original Compositions.

Founded by DR. Wm. SPARK, Late Organist, Town Hall, Leeds
Non-subscribers, 5/-each.   Subscription, 10/6 for 4 issues.

New Series, Volume, containing 160 large pages, bound in
cloth, 18s.

Part 12. New Series
1. IN MEMORIAM - - Rev. GEOF. C. RYLY. M.A., Mus. Bac. Oxon.
2. TOCCATA - - - - - - - - G. B. POLLERI.
3. OVERTURE from Epiphany - - - - ALFRED KING, M.D.

Part XI., New Series.
1. PRELUDE AND FUGUE with POSTLUDE - E. A. CHAMBERLAYNE.
2. PRELUDE AND FUGUE - - - - - - - F. YOUNG.
3. FUGUE - - - - - - - - ARCHIBALD DONALD.
4. FUGUE - - - - - - - - WILLIAM HOPE.

Part 10, New Series.
1. FUGUE - - - - - - - ARCHIBALD DONALD.
2. PRELUDE AND FUGUE with POSTLUDE - - E. A. CHAMBERLAYNE
3. PRELUDE AND FUGUE - - - - - - F. YOUNG.

Part 9, New Series.
1. ANDANTE CON MOTO - - - W. A. MONTGOMERY, L.T.C.L.
2. FANTASIA in E minor - - - - CUTHBERT HARRIS, Mus. B.,
3. POSTLUDE at Ephes. V. v. 19. Si tibi placeat, Mihi con displicet
  W. CONRADI, (Y. or B. 1816), Paul's Org. St. Church, Schwerin i/m Germany.
4. HARVEST MARCH - - - - - - - HENRY J. POOLE.

Part 8, New Series.
1. SCHERZO MINUET W MULLINEUX, Organist of the Town Hall, Bolton.
2. INTRODUCTION to the Hymn on the Passion, O Haupt Voll Blut und
  Wunden"
    W. CONRADI. Organist Paul's Church, Schwerin, Germany.
3. THESIS AND ANTITHESIS, or DISPUTE, APPEASEMENT, CONCILIATION
    W. CONRADI, Organist Paul's Church, Schwerin, Germany.
4. CARILLON in E - - CUTHBERT HARRIS, Mus.B., F.R.C.O., &c.
5. ANDANTE " Hope " - - - - - - INGLIS BERVON.
6. ORCHESTRAL MARCH in C
  JAMES CRAPPER. L. Mus., Organist of the Parish Ch., Kirkcudbright.

Part 7, New Series.
1. ANDANTE GRAZIOSO in G - - - CHAS. E. MELVILLE, F.R.C.O.
2. POLISH SONG, Arranged for the organ by PERCIVAL GARRETT. - CHOPIN.
3. INTRODUCTION, VARIATIONS, and FINALE on the Hymn Tune " Rock-
  ingham." - - - - - - - CH. R. FISHER, Mus. B.
4. TWO SOFT MOVEMENTS - - - - - W. C. FILBY, I.S.M.
      1. " Espérance."   2. " Tendrerse."
5. ANDANTE in A flat
  W. GRIFFITHS, Mus. B , Org. of St. Sepulchre Church, Northampton.
6. FUGUE, 4 Voice, 3 Subjects - - - - - DR. J. C. TILLY.

The Organist's Quarterly Journal (*cont.*).

Part 6, New Series.
1. Con Moto Moderato in C
   ORLANDO A. Mansfield, Mus.B., F.R.C.O.
2. Tempo di Menuetto - - - - - - - Geo. H. Ely.
3. Dirge in Memoriam, Reginald Adkins - J. E. Adkins, F.R.C.O.
4. Andante in F - - - - - - - R. H. Heath.
5. Aberystwyth Offertoire - - - - J. G. Mountford.
6. Andante in D (Prière) - - - E, Evelyn Barron, M.A.

Part 5, New Series.
1. Allegretto Scherzando in A flat - - - W. E. Ashmall.
2. Andante Religioso in G - - - - - Dr. J. Bradford.
3 March Pomposo in E flat - - - - Charles Darnton.
4. Andante Con Moto "Twilight" - - Ch. R. Fisher, Mus.B.
5. Minuet in F - - - - - - W E. Belcher, F.R.C.O

Part 4, New Series.
1. Andante Moderato - - - - - - - F. Read.
2. Prelude and Fugue in D minor - - - E. A. Chamberlayne.
3. Sketch - - - - - - - Arthur Geo. Colborn.
4. Fugue - - - - - - - - James Turpin.
5 Allegro - - - - - - - Charles H. Fisher.
6. Marche Mystique
   Theme by Roland, de Lassus.—A Relic of Ancient Times.

Part 3, New Series.
1. Minuet and Trio in F - - Ed. J. Bellerby, Mus. B., Oxon.
2. "Dunder " (" or French ") - - - John P. Attwater.
3. Adagio. An Elegy in G minor - - Chas. R. Fisher, Mus. B.
4. Andante. A major - - - - - - - F. Hone.
5. Allegro, D minor - - - - - - Geo. Minns (Ely).

Part 2, New Series.
1. Toccata Fantasia (*Study in C minor*) - - - E. T. Driffiel.
2. Andante Grazioso - - - - - - - W. Faulkes.
3. Marche Funebre - - - - - - Arthur Wanderer.
4. Andante Semplice - - - - - E. A. Chamberlayne.
5. Festal March - - - - - - A. W. Ketelbey.

Part 1, New Series.
1. Offertoire in A minor - - - Fred. W. Dal (Leipzig).
2. Second Fantasia on Scotch Airs - - - William Spark.
3. Adeste Fideles with Variations and Fugue) - Charles Hunt.
4. Intermezzo - - - - - G. Townshend Driffield.

Part 103, July 1894.
1. Postlude in G - - - - Frederick W. Holloway, F.C.O
2. Suite: No. 1, Prelude ; No. 2, Berceuse; No. 3, Toccata
   Laurent Parodi (Genoa
3. Nocturne - - - - - - - William Lockett.
4. Andante Pastorale in B minor Jacob Bradford; Mus. D., Oxon
5. Introductory Voluntary - - - Albert W. Ketelbey.
. Fugue - - - - - - - R. J. Rowe, L.R.A.M.

POPULAR AND COPYRIGHT MUSIC.

Full Music Size, Well Printed and Critically Correct.

ISSUED BY

2D. **WILLIAM REEVES.** **2**D.

(Postage ½d. each.)   (Postage ½d. each.)

VOCAL.

396.	Always do as I do	*Tinney*
174.	Angels at the Casement, A flat	*W. M. Hutchison*
105.	Banner of the King	*H. Fortesque*
172.	Barney O'Hea	*S. Lover*
224.	Bay of Biscay	*J. Davey*
181.	Border Lands (Sacred)	*Miss Lindsay*
180.	Borderer's Challenge	*H. J. Stark*
390.	Cat in the Chimney	*L. Kingsmill*
391.	Child's Good Morning	*O. Barri*
392.	Child's Good Night	*O. Barri*
383.	Come into the Garden Maud	*Balfe*
389.	Dawn of Heaven	*Buonetti*
188.	Diver, The	*E. J. Loder*
384.	God Save the King	*Dr. Jno. Bull*
226.	Hearts of Oak	*Dr. W. Boyce*
100.	Honey Are You True to Me (Coon Song)	*Lindsay Lennox*
213.	Lady Clara Vere de Vere	*Miss Lindsay*
227.	Last Rose of Summer	*Thos. Moore*
115.	Sharing the Burden	*J. E. Webster*
225.	Tom Bowling	*C. Dibdin*

PIANOFORTE.

118.	A la Valse	*Roeckel*
373.	Belgium Galop	*Smallwood*
122.	Berceuse	*Roeckel*
376.	Blumenlied	*Gustav Lang*
379.	Bridal Chorus and Wedding March	*Wagner*
142.	Charming Mazurka	*Gungl*
393.	Chinese Patrol March	*D. Pecorini*
243.	Cloches du Monastere	*Lefebure-Wely*
377.	Edelweiss	*Gustav Lange*
374.	Emmeline Galop	*Smallwood*
308.	Fille du Regiment	*Oesten*
167.	Flying Dutchman (La Vaisseau Fantome)	*Wagner*
244.	Forward March	*E. H. Sugg*
	Four Humoresques :	
206.	Valse in D, No. 1	*Grieg*
207.	Minuetto in A minor. No. 2	*Grieg*
208.	Allegretto, No. 3	*Grieg*
209.	Allegro Alla Burla, No. 4	*Grieg*
305.	French Air (easy)	*T. Valentine*
210.	Funeral March	*Grieg*
306.	German Air (easy)	*T. Valentine*
151.	Grand March of the Warriors	*H. V. Lewis*
125.	Il Corricolo Galop (easily arranged)	*L. Mullen*

Cheap Music (continued).—

304. Irish Air (easy) ... ... *T. Valentine*
303. Italian Air (easy) ... ... *T. Valentine*
133. Kassala Gavotte ... ... *H. Wilcock*
171. Khartoum Quick March ... ... *F. P. Rabottini*
246. Liberty Bell March ... ... *Sousa*
135. Little Dear Gavotte ... ... *F. Astrella*
162. Lohengrin ... ... *Wagner*
136. Maiden's Prayer ... ... *Badarazewska*
137. March in E flat ... ... *L. B. Mallett*
140. May-Day Galopade ... ... *J. Gungl*
141. Mazurka ... ... *Badarazewska*
143. Melodie ... ... *Roeckel*
247. Melody in F ... ... *Rubinstein*
211. Minuetto .. .. *Grieg*
163. Mountain Echo March ... ... *G. Gariboldi*
385. Narcissus ... ... *Nevin*
147. Placid Stream ... ... *Smallwood*
103. Queenie (Intermezzo) ... ... *P. D'Orsay*
165. Rienzi ... ... *Wagner*
148. Scherzino ... ... *Roeckel*
301. Scotch Air (easy) ... ... *T. Valentine*
375. Seasons Galop ... ... *Smallwood*
196. Silvery Echoes ... ... *Blake*
394. Soldiers' Chorus (Faust) ... ... *Gounod*
381. Sonatina in F ... ... *Beethoven*
380. Sonata in G ... ... *Beethoven*
302. Spanish Air (easy) ... ... *T. Valentine*
378. Stephanie Gavotte ... ... *A. Czibulka*
166. Tannhauser ... ... *Wagner*
150. Tarantella ... ... *L. B. Mallett*
290. Washington Post March (easy arrange-
    ment by Edwin Lausdale) ... *J. P. Sousa*
291. Woodland Echoes ... ... *Wyman*

DANCE.

388. Amorosa Mazurka ... ... *A. H. Oswald*
387. Blue Bells Schottische ... ... *S. Leslie*
382. British Army Polka ... ... *Alec Carlton*
161. Cosmopolitan Quadrille ... ... *L. Gautier*
127. Cyprus Polka ... ... *Scotson Clark*
101. Electric Waltz ... ... *H. Klein*
397. Esmeralda Waltz ... ... *S. Osborne*
395. Fancy Dress Ball Quadrille ... ... *Rosenberg*
386. Horse Guards Schottische ... ... *S. Leslie*
102. Lucifer Polka ... ... *H. Klein*
144. Munich Polka ... ... *Jos. Gungl*
366. Roseland Waltz ... ... *Marietta Lena*

PIANO DUETS.

156. March of the Cameron Men ... ... *A. Mullen*
155. Marche des Croates ... ... *A. Mullen*
159. Minnie, or Lilly Dale ... ... *A. Mullen*

VIOLIN.

170. March St. Olave ... ... *F. James*

Books on Freemasonry

Published by W. REEVES,
83 Charing Cross Road, W.C

12mo, red cloth, gilt, 323 pp., 3/6.

Carlile (R.), Manual of Freemasonry, containing the First Three Degrees, The Royal Arch and Knights' Templar Druids, The Degrees of Mark Man, Mark Master, Architect, Grand Architect., etc., etc.

12mo, blue cloth, gilt, 374 pp., 3/6.

Fellows (J.), Mysteries of Freemasonry; or, An Exposition of the Religious Dogmas and Customs of the Ancient Egyptians; showing, from the origin, nature and objects of the rites and ceremonies of remote antiquity, their identity with the Order of Modern Masonry, with some remarks on the Metamorphosis of Apuleius. *with numerous illustrative woodcuts.*

12mo, green cloth, gilt, 254 pp., 3/6.

Ritual and Illustrations of Freemasonry, *accompanied by very numerous engravings,* and a Key to the Phi Beta Kappa.

8vo, sewed, 26 pp., 1/-

Investigation into the Cause of the Hostility of the Church of Rome to Freemasonry, and an Inquiry into Freemasonry as it Was, and Is: with a Criticism as to how far the Order fulfils its Functions, by the Author of "The Text Book of Freemasonry."

Post 8vo, sewed, 48 pp., 1/-

Joachin and Boaz; or, an Authentic Key to the Door of Freemasonry, both Ancient and Modern.

Post 8vo, sewed, 50 pp., 1/-

Three Distinct Knocks at the Door of the Most Ancient Freemasonry

8vo, sewed, 1/-

The Origin of Freemasonry, or the 1717 Theory Exploded by C. J. Paton, 8vo. 1s.

8vo, paper, 2/6 (post free 3/-)

Weisse (John A.), The Obelisk of Freemasonry, according to the Discoveries of Belzoni and Commander Gorringe: also Egyptian Symbols compared with those discovered in American Mounds.

Fifth thousand, 12mo, cloth 1/-

Pocket Lexicon of Freemasonry, by W. J. Morris, 18° P.D.D.G.M., St. Lawrence, District and Past Inspector Gen. Royal and Select Masters.

12mo, cloth, 62 pp., 2/-

Fox (T. L.), Freemasonry; An Account of the Early History of Freemasonry in England, with Illustrations of the Principles and Precepts advocated by that Institution.

The above POST FREE on receipt of remittance for price named.

Books on Freemasonry

Published by W. REEVES,
83, Charing Cross Road, W.C.

12mo, blue cloth, red edges, 270 pp. 5/-

Text Book of Freemasonry; a Complete Handbook of Instruction to all the Workings in the Various Mysteries and Ceremonies of CRAFT MASONRY, containing the Entered Apprentice, Fellow-craft, and Master Mason's degrees; the Ceremony of Installation of the W. Master and Officers of the Lodge, together with the whole of the Three Lectures; also the Ceremony of Exhaltation in the Supreme Order of the Holy Royal Arch, a Selection of Masonic Songs, etc., *illustrated with four engravings of the* **TRACING BOARDS**, by " A Member of the Craft," new and revised edition.

Ditto, Ditto, on thin paper, bound in leather pocket-book style, 5s.

The Three Tracing Boards, in 12mo, cloth line, 1s. 6d.

Ditto, Larger Size. roy. 8vo, 4 plates, 1s. 6d.

Post 8vo, cloth, 278 pp., 10/- (or crimson calf limp. gilt edges, 15/-

Text Book of Advanced Freemasonry, containing for the self-Instruction of Candidates, the COMPLETE RITUALS of the HIGHER DEGREES, viz., Royal Ark Mariners, Mark Master, Royal Arch, Red Cross of Rome and Constantinople, Knights' Templar and Rose Croix de Heredom; also Monitorial Instructions on the 30th to the 33rd and last degree of Freemasonry, to which are added Historical Introductions and Explanatory remarks by the Author of the " Text Book."

8vo, cloth, 300 pp., 3/6

HONE (William), Ancient Mysteries described, especially the English Miracle Plays founded on the Apocryphal New Testament Story, extant among the unpublished MSS.in the British Museum, including notices of Ecclesiastical shows and Festivals of Fools and Asses, the English Boy Bishop, Descent into Hell, the Lord Mayor's Show, the Guildhall Giants, Christmas Carols, etc., with engravings and Index.

8vo, cloth, 3/6

HONE (William) The Apocryphal New Testament, being all the Gospels, Epistles and other pieces now extant attributed in the first four centuries to Jesus Christ, his Apostles and their Companions and not included in the New Testament by its compilers.

Any of the above sent POST FREE *upon receipt of Remittance for price named.*

The Set of 15 numbers 2/6 post free.
Or 2d. each (Post free 2½d.)

PARISH CHURCH MUSIC.

A Collection of Original, Practical, Modern Compositions—
Tunes, Canticles, Chants, etc., for use in " Choirs
and Places where they Sing." :—

No. 1.—Six Tunes to the Hymn "NEARER MY GOD TO THEE," including the Three Prize Tunes.

No. 2.—Six Tunes to the Hymn "LEAD KINDLY LIGHT," including the Three Prize Tunes.

No. 3.—Four Tunes to the Hymn, "JESUS, LOVER OF MY SOUL," including the Three Prize Tunes.

No. 4.—Five Tunes to the Hymn, "LO! HE COMES WITH CLOUDS DESCENDING," including the Three Prize Tunes.

No. 5.—Five Tunes to the Hymn, "I HEARD THE VOICE OF JESUS SAY," including the Three Prize Tunes.

No. 6.—Six Tunes to the Hymn, "FOR THEE, O DEAR, DEAR COUNTRY," including the Three Prize Tunes.

No. 7.—Four Tunes to the Hymn, "O LOVE WHO FORMEDST ME TO WEAR."

No. 8.—Six Tunes to the Hymn, "THE KING OF LOVE," including Three Prize Tunes.

No. 9.—Ten Tunes to the Hymn, "ABIDE WITH ME," including Three Prize Tunes.

No. 10.—Ferial Confession, "STORY OF THE CROSS," Choir Prayers with Antiphon, by G. E. Lake.

No. 11.—Five Tunes to the Hymn, "ROCK OF AGES," including Three Prize Tunes.

No. 12.—Six Quadruple Chants for the "TE DEUM," including the Three Prize Tunes.

No. 13.—Ten Tunes to the Hymn, "SUN OF MY SOUL," including Three Prize Tunes.

No. 14.—Ten Tunes to "JERUSALEM THE GOLDEN," including Three Prize Tunes.

No. 15.—Eleven Tunes to the Hymn, "HARK, HARK, MY SOUL," including Three Prize Tunes.

W. REEVES, 83, CHARING CROSS ROAD, W.C.

THE VIOLIN TIMES,

Monthly, 2d.,
(by post 2½d.)

Edited by E. POLONASKI.

Subscription, 2s. 6d., per Year   -   -   Abroad, 3s.

VOLS. 1 TO 8, BOUND, PRICE 6/- EACH.

Covers for binding
2s. each.
Index 2d. each.

Illustrated Supplements have appeared Including the following (2½d. each.)

PORTRAITS.

VOL 8.
Prof. and Mrs. Holloway
and Family
Eugene Polonaski
Hugo Kupferschmidt
Dr. Joachim.
Anton Schumacher
William Christ Basle
M. Coward-Klee
Dettmar Dressel
The Joachim Quartet
Kubelik
C. M. Hawcroft

VOL. 7.
W. A. Mozart
Miss Kate Lee
R. Peckotsch
Gordon Tanner
Eugene Meier
W. V. Fisher
Paganini
T. B. Parsons
Joseph   Guarnerius   del
Gesu Violin, 1733

VOL. 6.
Pierre Baillot
C. A. de Beriot
J. R. Bingley
Ole Bull
Arcangelo Corelli

PORTRAITS (continued.)

Ferdinand David
Elderhorst Quartette
H. Wilhelm Ernst
Miss Muriel Handley
Miska Hauser
N. Paganini
Louis Spohr
A. Stradivarius
H. Vieuxtemps
G. Viotti

VOL. 5.
T. G. Briggs
Cologne Gurzenich Quartette
Wm. Henley
Miss Leonora Jackson
J. Koh-Alblas
A. Oppenheim (violinist)
A. Oppenheim (pianist)
Mdlle. Jeanette Orloff
Dr. H. Pudor
C. L. Walger

W. E. Whitehouse
Miss Gladys May Hooley
J. Harold Henry
Adolphe Pollitzer
Mdlle. Edith Smith
John Dunn
Heinrich Maria Hain
Edina Bligh

PORTRAITS (continued.

I. B. Poznanski
Rene Ortmans
A. Simonetti
W. Ten Have
Mdlle. Wietrowitz
Miss Hildegard Werner
Fred Furnace
Miss Kathleen Thomas
M. Césare Thomson
F. Whiteley
H. Lvell Tayler
Stanley W. G. Barfoot
G. de Angelis
Marcello Rossi

FACSIMILES AND PICTURES.

Paganini on his Death-bed
Letter of Ch. de Bériot
Letter of Camillo Sivori
Defeasance of a bond by
Roger Wade Crowder
Viola di Gamba by Carlo
Bergonzi, 1713
Facsimile Labels in Nos.
32, 34, 35, 37, 505, ,58
Lira da Gamba, by Linarolo,
reproduction of Painting
by Tintoretto
David Techler's Viola
Stradivari's Scroll
Jacob Stainer's House

Price One Shilling (Cloth 1/6)

Notes on **CONDUCTORS**

AND

CONDUCTING.

*New and Enlarged
Edition.*

BY

T. R. CROGER, F.R.G.S., F.Z.S.,

Fellow of the Philharmonic Society,
Conductor of the Nonconformist Choir Union Orchestra, and
Hon. Sec. Nonconformist Choir Union.

*With three Full-page Illustrations of the various " Beats,"
and Plan of an Orchestra.*

" A mine of good things."—*Musical Opinion.*
" One of the best guides to conducting."—
Piano and Music Trades Review.
" Calculated to be eminently useful."—*The Strad.*
"Brightly written and companionable."—*Musical Times.*
" We very cordially advise all young conductors to read this
instructive work."—*Nonconformist Musical Journal,*
" To these (village Conductors) the author's many hints and
picturesque category of ' Do not's ' cannot fail to be of value."
—*Musical News.*
" A little book which is as full of good things as an egg is full
of meat . . . and in this book budding Conductors, and
full-blown ones also, will find food for thought. *Buy the book !* "
—*Musical Opinion.*
" Mr. T. R. Croger has sat under many batons during the last
thirty years, and he chats about the ways and needs of Conductors
very pleasantly. . . . He is interesting, and to the point."
—*The Musical Herald.*
" Without going into a long description of what conducting
is, and how to do it, we may confidently say that the work before
us is one of the best of guides to the art of conducting an Orchestra or Choir."—*Piano and Music Trades' Journal.*
" Great Conductors are born, not made ; still, there are thou-
sands who have to wield the baton in Church, Chapel, and other
Choirs, and would be the better for a little schooling. Mr. Croger
gives here some good practical hints."—*Monthly Musical Record.*
" Some truthful illustrations of choir competitions and public
performances are very humorous. . . . We advise all to read
and study this little book, and we feel sure much good will be
the result to those who require guidance in this direction."
—*The Minim.*